The
Little Book
of Cat Magic

Bobbie Hodges

About the Author

Deborah Blake is the award-winning author of *The Goddess is in the Details*, *Everyday Witchcraft*, and numerous other books from Llewellyn, along with her *Everyday Witch Tarot* kit. She has published articles in Llewellyn annuals, and her ongoing column, "Everyday Witchcraft," is featured in *Witches & Pagans*.

When not writing, Deborah runs the Artisans' Guild, a cooperative shop she founded with a friend in 1999, and also works as a jewelry maker, tarot reader, and energy healer. She lives in a 130-year-old farmhouse in rural upstate New York with various cats who supervise all her activities, magickal and mundane. She can be found online at Facebook, Twitter, and www.deborahblakeauthor.com.

The
Little Book
of Cat Magic

Spells, Charms
& Tales

Deborah Blake

Llewellyn Publications
WOODBURY, MINNESOTA

FIRST EDITION
First Printing, 2018

Cover illustration by Lisa Parker
Interior illustrations by Alice Rosen

Llewellyn Publications is a registered trademark
of Llewellyn Worldwide Ltd.

The Library of Congress Cataloging-in-Publication Data is pending.

ISBN 978-0-7387-5323-2

Llewellyn Publications
A Division of Llewellyn Worldwide Ltd.
2143 Wooddale Drive
Woodbury, MN 55125-2989
www.llewellyn.com

Printed in the United States of America

To all my cats, past and present. Thank you for sharing my life with me—I can't imagine living it without you. Most of all, to Magic the Cat (Queen of the Universe) who inspired every witchy book, especially this one. I miss you (and your brother Mystic) with every atom of my being. Thank you for being my friend and my familiar. I know your mother Minerva is happy to have you both back by her side again. Have fun bossing everyone around in the Summerlands.

And to the woman most likely to be nominated a cat, my wonderful editor Elysia Gallo. Thanks as always for your helpful suggestions and your patience with my occasional bouts of twitching. Just remember—my writing this book was your idea. You have no one to blame but yourself!

Contents

6: *Cat Health* 85

7: *Love and Loss* 101

8: *Connecting with Your Cat* 115

9: The Cat as Familiar 137

10: Power Animals 153

13: Channeling Your Inner Cat   207

The Magical Cat

If you are worthy of its affection, a cat will
be your friend, but never your slave.

• • • • • • • • •
THEOPHILE GAUTIER

. . .

If you have ever had a cat (I won't say owned, because no one ever really owns a cat), you already know they have a special magic. Not that all animals aren't special, but cats are even more special than the rest. If you don't believe me, just ask one.

Witches and cats have had a close connection down through the centuries, and cats have been associated with magic and spiritual matters in many different cultures. There's a good reason for this. Cats are mysterious; they seem to know things they shouldn't possibly be able to know. They are uncanny at times, with eyes that glow, finding their way in the dark and into places it seems they shouldn't be able to fit. They disappear and reappear at will, and only come when called if they are in the mood.

And a cat's mood can be as changeable as the moon. One minute they're giving you the cold shoulder for some unforgivable offense and the next minute they're cuddled up on your lap, purring as if someone had turned on a motor. That purr is magical too, able to soothe and calm and comfort the lucky human who hears it.

Kittens are probably one of the cutest sights on earth. Their big eyes and wide yawns amuse us as they tumble over their own feet and climb up the curtains. But even adult cats can be adorable and playful—when they're not napping, eating, or being sophisticated and magical.

Cats are more than simply decorative and entertaining. They have long coexisted with humans as pest control specialists (try to find a farm that doesn't have at least a few to keep the mice and rat population in check), early morning alarm clocks, and food tasters. And all joking aside, they are faithful, loving companions, snugglers extraordinaire, and, on occasion, familiars.

I have had cats since I was a child, and I can't imagine my life without them. Since I came to my practice as a Witch, they have taken on an even greater role, if that is possible. Not all cats are familiars (only one of mine, the aptly named Magic the Cat, Queen of the Universe, has been a true familiar), but many times they have shown interest in my magical work or displayed that special intuition cats seem to have.

This book is for all those who love and are loved by cats, especially those who have a magical bent. It will give you tools to help your feline companions, useful spells for many cat-centric issues, and tips for both living with and practicing magic with your cats. Scattered throughout the book will also be quotes and poems and sage advice from my own Magic the Cat. (She insisted, and if you have ever tried arguing with a cat, you know there is simply no point.)

We both hope you will find some fun ideas, helpful suggestions, and amusing tidbits within its pages. Try not to chew on them.

A Note About Using Cat Components

Some of the spells in this book call for a bit of your cat's fur, claws, or whiskers. Obviously, these should not be taken off the cat in any way that would harm it. Cats naturally shed their claw sheaths and their whiskers, and oh, boy, do they shed their fur. You can sweep that up and use it, or brush your cat (which he or she will undoubtedly appreciate) if you want fur that is cleaner.

Never pull out a cat's whiskers or clip an entire claw, although you can use the tiny tips you get when you trim a cat's nails. If you can't safely get these components, you can always substitute a picture of your cat instead.

Most Commonly Used Spell Ingredients in This Book

Many of the spells in this book use the same basic ingredients (besides those your cat contributes), so if you want to stock up, you can get a few from the following list. Keep in mind that while these may be the optimum components, you can always substitute whatever feels right to you or use a white candle instead of another color or simply do the spell without them. Spell ingredients serve the purpose of focusing your will and your intent, and they are fun to use, but your own mind and heart are the only tools you truly need—well, and a cat, of course.

- tiger's-eye tumbled stone and chips, quartz crystal, or agate or jasper small stones (you can find these at jewelry supply stores, online, or at some New Age or Pagan shops)
- catnip, valerian, or rosemary (dried and fresh)
- sea salt
- water
- sage smudge stick
- white, brown, green, light blue, and pink candles
- picture of your cat
- statue or picture of Bast or other cat-related deity
- small cloth bags or squares of fabric plus ribbon, yarn, or thread

CHAPTER 1

Cats Through History

*Thousands of years ago, cats were worshipped
as gods. Cats have never forgotten this.*

— TERRY PRATCHETT

• • •

As any cat will tell you, they have had an important place in history since the first cat ancestor slunk out of the forest and sat down next to a human's fire, no doubt acting as if they had always been there waiting to be fed.

Ever since that time, they have been associated with witches and magic and all things mystical, as well as being a part of our culture and our lives. There is evidence that wildcats first lived among people over 100,000 years ago in Mesopotamia. Cats, dogs, and other animals probably started actually being domesticated there around 12,000 BCE. It is thought that cats were originally used for pest control, although I think it is equally probable that cats were the ones doing the domesticating and just chased mice because they felt like it.

From then on, cats have played an important role in a number of countries and cultures. Here are a few of the best-known examples.

Happy is the home with at least one cat.

Cats in Egypt

For a long time, it was believed that cats originated in Egypt. Certainly that is where they first rose to power in their attempt to take over the world. (Kidding. Sort of.) Ancient Egyptians were famous for their devotion to cats, including having a cat goddess, Bastet.

Cats were considered sacred. It was illegal to export them, and anyone who killed a cat was put to death. The city of Bubastis, which meant "house of Bastet," contained a large temple complex where cats were mummified after they died. People who lost a cat signified their deep mourning by shaving off their eyebrows and continuing to mourn until they grew back.

The very name "cat" comes from the North African word *quattah*, as do the variations in other languages, including the French *chat*, the German *katze*, and the Italian *gatto*.

Cats in India

Cats feature in two of the most famous stories from ancient India. In the *Mahabharata* there is an unlikely friendship between a cat named Lomasa and a mouse named Palita (the original Tom and Jerry?), who save each other from death and have deep discussions of a philosophical nature. In the *Ramayana* the god Indra disguises himself as a cat to escape the wrath of an angry husband when Indra was caught having sex with his wife. (Apparently the disguise didn't work, and the god ended up being cursed to lose some of his manly parts. Ouch.)

Cats in Persia

It is said that the prophet Muhammad loved cats. There is a famous story that tells of how Muhammad's favorite cat, Meuzza, fell asleep on his arm, and rather than disturb the animal, Muhammad cut the sleeve off of his robe. Another tale says that the tabby cat got its "M" marking on its forehead when the prophet laid his hand on Meuzza's head in blessing.

There is also a Persian tale that tells of how, using magic, the cat was created as a gift for the great hero Rustum. I'll tell you that story in the next chapter.

Cats in Japan and China

The Chinese have a myth about cats at the beginning of the world. (Of course cats were there—where else would they have been?) The Japanese saw cats as guardians of valuable books and sometimes the home in general. Cats often had their own pagodas, and in early Japan (around the tenth century CE) only the nobility could afford to have one.

One of the most popular and readily recognized images of a cat is the maneki neko, or beckoning cat, who sits with one paw raised. Also known as a "lucky cat," the figure represents the goddess of mercy and is considered to be good luck. I have a few of them in my own house, as they are popular gifts for cat lovers to this day. (My favorite is a bobble-head lucky cat that my lovely editor Elysia gave to me. It sits by my desk and whenever I read something depressing online, I give it a little bop and it cheers me right up.)

Cats in Rome and Greece

By the time cats reached Rome and Greece, they were more likely to be treated as pets rather than kept for their usefulness as pest control (the Romans and Greeks used weasels for that, believe it or not). The Greek playwright Aristophanes is thought to have originated the phrase "the cat did it" as part of his comic plays. We still use that one in my house…

Greek mythology, however, also may have been the origin of the first negative association between cats and witches. There is one particular myth in which a woman was turned into a cat by Hera and banished into the underworld to serve Hecate, the goddess of witches, and darkness, among other things.

Cats in Europe:
The Good, the Bad, and the Ugly

Perhaps in reaction to the positive view of cats among the pagan peoples of Ireland and Scotland, who saw them as magical, eventually the Catholic Church began to view cats as evil, associated with both witches and the devil. In the 1200s Pope Gregory IX issued a papal bull (a kind of official church announcement) saying that cats were evil and in league with Satan, and people began killing them all across Europe, especially black cats. (Magic the Cat would like you to know she is particularly indignant about this.) Women who had cats, in particular elderly women, also fared badly. In was a dark time.

Thankfully, cats regained their popularity during the Victorian Age (1837–1901), thanks to Queen Victoria herself. Previously a dog person, the queen apparently became intrigued with cats through the era's fascination with Egyptology. She adopted two blue Persian cats and made them a part of her court. Because she was popular with the common people, this caused a resurgence in the desire to own cats. The felines were back. You knew they would be.

Eventually this interest spread to America, especially through the most widely read magazine of the time, *Godey's Lady's Book*. Cats, which were thought to have come to the United States around 1749, surged in popularity, and the rest is history.

Cats have it all: admiration, an endless sleep, and company only when they want it.

ROD MCKUEN

Magic the Cat

What all this stuffy history doesn't tell you is that cats have been influencing important humans since the beginning of time. For instance, did you know that Florence Nightingale, who invented nursing, was a cat lady? She had over sixty cats during her lifetime. She probably learned everything she knew about making people feel better from them. President Jimmy Carter had a cat named Misty Malarky Ying Yang. No, I am not making that up. Writer Ernest Hemingway had eight cats, named Alley Cat, Crazy Christian, Ecstasy, F. Puss, Fats, Friendless Brother, Dillinger, and Pilar. Seriously…writers are weird. John Lennon had a cat named Elvis. Think about that one for a minute. My point is that writers, musicians, politicians, and all sorts of other famous people had cats whispering in their ears. I'm pretty sure that's why they ended up famous. Just pointing out the obvious.

The Duel

EUGENE FIELD

The gingham dog and the calico cat
Side by side on the table sat;
'Twas half-past twelve, and (what do you think!)
Nor one nor t' other had slept a wink!
The old Dutch clock and the Chinese plate
Appeared to know as sure as fate
There was going to be a terrible spat.

(I wasn't there; I simply state
What was told to me by the Chinese plate!)

The gingham dog went "bow-wow-wow!"
And the calico cat replied "mee-ow!"
The air was littered, an hour or so,
With bits of gingham and calico,
While the old Dutch clock in the chimney-place
Up with its hands before its face,
For it always dreaded a family row!

(Now mind: I'm only telling you
What the old Dutch clock declares is true!)

The Chinese plate looked very blue,
And wailed, "Oh, dear! what shall we do!"
But the gingham dog and the calico cat
Wallowed this way and tumbled that,
Employing every tooth and claw
In the awfullest way you ever saw—
And, oh! how the gingham and calico flew!
     (*Don't fancy I exaggerate—*
     I got my news from the Chinese plate!)

Next morning, where the two had sat
They found no trace of dog or cat;
And some folks think unto this day
That burglars stole that pair away!
But the truth about the cat and pup
Is this: they ate each other up!
Now what do you really think of that!
     (*The old Dutch clock it told me so,*
     And that is how I came to know.)

CHAPTER 2

Cat Myths, Folklore, and Tales

*I believe cats to be spirits come to
earth. A cat, I am sure, could walk on
a cloud without coming through.*

• • • • • •
JULES VERNE

17

• • •

There are many myths and plenty of folklore that revolve around cats. Some of it is magical, some sensible, and some just plain silly. Here is a fun assortment I came across while researching this book, some of which I'd heard of before and some of which was new to me. Try reading them out loud to your cat to find out which ones they approve of and which they think are utter nonsense. I'm sure they'll find some way to let you know. Plus, here are some fascinating facts you might not know about the animal who rules your house—I mean, with whom you share your home.

Fascinating Facts

- A group of cats is called a clowder.
- Cats are the most popular pet in the United States: there are about eight pet cats to every seven dogs. But only 24 percent of cats who enter animal shelters are adopted.
- Cats sleep 70 percent of their lives.
- In tigers and tabbies, the middle of the tongue is covered in backward-pointing spines, used for breaking off and grabbing meat. But they can't taste sweetness. (That's just sad!)

- Cats have over twenty muscles that control their ears. Hearing is the strongest of cat's senses. They can hear sounds as high as 64 kHz—compared with humans, who can hear only as high as 20 kHz. This probably explains why they can hear the can opener from wherever they are. Cats can move their ears 180 degrees and move them separately.

- When cats make a face, they are sometimes tasting the air. They have an extra organ that, with some breathing control, allows them to taste-sense the air.

- Cats have inferior daytime sight, but during the night they need seven times less light than humans to see.

- Owning a cat can lessen the risk of stroke and heart attack by a third. They have also detected cancer in their owners. The frequency of a domestic cat's purr is the same at which muscles and bones repair themselves.

- The world's largest cat measured 48.5 inches long.

- Female cats are typically right-pawed while male cats are typically left-pawed.

- Cats make more than 100 different sounds. Dogs make around ten, thus proving the cat's superiority once again.

- Cats use their whiskers to detect if they can fit through a space.

- A cat's brain is 90 percent similar to a human's. Cats and humans have nearly identical sections of the brain that control emotion. And a cat's cerebral cortex (the part of the brain in charge of cognitive information processing) has 300 million neurons, compared with a dog's 160 million. Cats also have a longer-term memory than dogs, especially when they learn by actually doing rather than simply seeing. (Maybe this explains why they hold a grudge longer.)

- Cats have five toes on their front paws and four on the back, unless they are a polydactyl (a cat with extra toes). Polydactyl cats are also referred to as "Hemingway cats" because the author was so fond of them.

- Abraham Lincoln kept four cats in the White House. When asked if her husband had any hobbies, Mary Todd Lincoln is said to have replied, "Cats."

- A cat can jump up to six times its length.

- Cats only sweat through their feet.

- A cat's nose is ridged with a unique pattern, just like a human fingerprint.

- Cats have scent glands along their tail, forehead, lips, chin, and the underside of their front paws. When they rub against people or furniture, they are marking their territory. Yes, you are your cat's territory.

Mythology, Lore, and Legends
From Around the World

The color of a cat's coat could make a big difference in its life, depending on where in the world it lived. The Irish thought a tortoiseshell cat brought good luck, but black cats in Celtic lore were considered evil and were often killed. The Cat Sìth, a Celtic legend common in Scotland, was thought to be either a fairy creature or possibly a witch who appeared as a large black cat with a spot on its chest. It was said that the Cat Sìth could steal a dead person's soul and that leaving milk out for it on Samhain (Halloween) would ensure that it blessed the household instead of cursed it.

The Japanese also thought that tortoiseshell cats brought good luck, especially if they were tortoiseshell and white. They also believed that a black spot on a cat indicated that the cat carried the soul of a departed ancestor. In Buddhist, Burmese, and Siamese cultures, cats were thought to host the holiest souls on their way to paradise.

Another legend from this area of the world said that the darker patches on the necks of Siamese cats were the thumbprints of the gods, showing where they picked up the cats to admire them. No wonder Siamese cats have so much attitude!

Blue cats are highly valued in Russia. Actually a silvery blueish gray, the Russian blue is a distinctive breed known for its thick, silky fur. It was also considered to bring good fortune to a new couple if a cat moved into their new home with them.

The Russian Karelian, a long-haired bobtailed cat, was believed to be an enchanted princess.

In Britain, tortoiseshells were considered to be bad luck. Some folks thought white cats were bad luck and black cats beneficial, while others saw it the other way around. It was said that if a black cat crossed your path, it meant you hadn't offended the witch it belonged to and she would pass you by.

Black cats often have been unfairly tagged as associated with evil. This is probably because black was considered to be the color of night and darkness, and therefore frightening. Early myths gave black cats a bad name. Hebrew tales about Adam's first wife, Lilith, later said to be a vampire, told of her turning into a huge black cat who preyed on helpless infants by stealing their breath. (The old wives' tale about cats stealing baby's breath persists to this day.)

During the Middle Ages, cats were believed to have evil powers (with or without a witch companion), and some thought their teeth were venomous and their breath could infect human lungs with tuberculosis, known as consumption. They could also make beer go sour. That would be a pity!

During the sixteenth century, Italians believed that if a black cat jumped on your bed while you were ill, it meant that you would die. On the other hand, in parts of France a strange black cat meowing on your doorstep meant you would marry soon. (I'm not sure what it meant if you were already married!) And Buddhist lore suggested that a dark-colored cat would bring gold in your future, whereas a polydactyl (extra-toed) cat meant good fortune.

Cat Tales

How Cats Got Their Purrs

There is an old European tale that says that long ago, a princess was given an impossible task. She was ordered to spin 10,000 skeins of linen thread in a month or else the prince she loved would be put to death. The princess was locked in a room with only her three cats for company. In desperation, she asked them to help her. The three cats and the princess worked night and day and finished the task, spinning and spinning. The cats' reward was the ability to purr, a sound somewhat like the whirring of the spinning wheel.

How Persian Cats Were Created

According to an ancient Persian tale, cats were created from magic. Rustum, a great Persian hero, was on one of his adventures when he saved a magician from a band of thieves and gave the older man shelter in his tent. As they sat by the fire under the stars, the magician asked Rustum how he could reward the hero for saving him. Rustum answered that he already had everything he could desire: the warmth and comfort of the fire, the smell of the smoke, and the beauty of the stars above them.

So the magician took a handful of the smoke and mixed it with the flames, then brought down two bright stars. He then kneaded them together and blew on them, creating a small smoky-gray kitten with bright eyes like the twinkling stars and a tongue that flickered like the flames. This was how the first Persian cat came to be.

Chinese Cat Creation Myth

The Chinese say that when the world began, the gods appointed cats to make sure that things were running smoothly and gave them the gift of speech to help them communicate clearly. But cats were much more interested in sleeping under cherry trees and chasing the falling blossoms. They couldn't be bothered to be in charge of the world and suggested to the gods that perhaps humans might be better at the job. The gods were disappointed but agreed to take the power of speech away from cats and give it to humans instead. Alas, humans turned out to be not very good at the job either. We were allowed to keep the power of speech, but cats were put back in charge, where they remain to this day.

How Pussy Willows Came to Be

According to an old Polish legend, a mother cat was crying at the bank of the river in which her babies were drowning. The willows at the river's edge dropped their long, graceful branches into the waters to rescue the tiny kittens who had fallen into the river while chasing butterflies. The kittens gripped on tightly to their branches and were brought to shore safely. Each springtime since, the willow branches sprout tiny fur-like buds at their tips where the tiny kittens once clung.

The Owl and the Pussy-cat

EDWARD LEAR

The Owl and the Pussy-cat went to sea
    In a beautiful pea-green boat,
They took some honey, and plenty of money.
    Wrapped up in a five-pound note.
The Owl looked up to the stars above,
    And sang to a small guitar,
"O lovely Pussy! O Pussy, my love,
What a beautiful Pussy you are,
      You are
      You are!
What a beautiful Pussy you are!"

Pussy said to the Owl, "You elegant fowl!
    How charmingly sweet you sing!
O let us be married! too long we have tarried:
    But what shall we do for a ring?"

They sailed away, for a year and a day,

To the land where the Bong-Tree grows

And there in a wood a Piggy-wig stood

With a ring at the end of his nose,

His nose,

His nose,

With a ring at the end of his nose.

"Dear Pig, are you willing to sell for one shilling

Your ring?" Said the Piggy, "I will."

So they took it away, and were married next day

By the Turkey who lives on the hill.

They dined on mince, and slices of quince,

Which they ate with a runcible spoon;

And hand in hand, on the edge of the sand,

They danced by the light of the moon,

The moon,

The moon,

They danced by the light of the moon.

CHAPTER 3

Cat Deities

I love cats because I love my home; and little
by little, they become its visible soul.

• • • • • • •
JEAN COCTEAU

• • •

There are a number of deities who are specifically associated with cats and those who love them. Bast is probably the best known, but there are others as well. Here is a quick run-down of the more popular cat-related deities. I suggest that if you want to work with one in particular, you do some more exploration on your own to learn as much as you can and figure out which deity suits you (and your familiar) best. Or, of course, you could let your cat choose.

Ai Apaec

The chief god of the pre-Inca civilization known as the Mochica, Ai Apaec was often depicted as an old man with a wrinkled face, long fangs, catlike whiskers, said to have evolved from an ancient cat god. He sometimes assumed the form of a tomcat.

A fierce protector of his people, Ai Apaec was both feared and adored (much like a cat, really). He is sometimes associated with jaguars. He was the patron god of hunters, fishermen, farmers, and healers. Call on Ai Apaec for protection or help with your garden or anything else to do with putting food on your table.

Bast

Bast is an Egyptian goddess often pictured with the body of a woman and the head of a cat, wearing gold earrings and a collar. Black cats are especially sacred to her, and it isn't uncommon to find statues of regal black Egyptian-looking cats to represent her on an altar. Bast is associated with motherhood, fertility, love, sex, and music. If you want a protector for new kittens or a new baby, Bast is a good goddess to call on. She is also called Bastet, Pasht, and Ubastet.

Other Egyptian deities, including Mut, Hathor, and Sekhmet (who some saw as a lioness form of Bastet) were also associated with wildcats. Bastet originally was associated with the lioness but eventually softened and was seen as the goddess of domestic cats and kittens, sometimes called "the mother of all cats."

Bast had a festival in her honor in the spring, usually in mid-April, so this would be an appropriate time to set out offerings to her. Although statues of Bast usually depict a black cat, it is likely that Egyptian cats were often buff, golden, or reddish in color. Call on her for love, sexuality, fertility, motherhood, or anything to do with your own cat's needs.

Freya

A Norse goddess, her name means "the Lady," and she is associated with love, beauty, sex, war, death, gold, magic, and shapeshifting. Freya is known for numerous things, including Brisingamen (her necklace of amber and rubies), a cloak made from falcon feathers, and her chariot, which was pulled by two massive cats who were a gift from Thor. She was quite fond of cats and was sometimes known as the Mistress of Cats. Farmers wishing to curry her favor would put milk out for stray cats. (That would get them the cats' favor too, no doubt.)

Freya ruled over Fólkvangr, where half of those who died in battle went, and she was the leader of the Valkyries. It was said that when Freya and the Valkyries rode to battle, they caused the magical flickering lights in the sky known as the aurora borealis, or northern lights. She comforted the dying and carried them to the afterworld.

Also a goddess of love and sexuality, Freya was said to be irresistibly beautiful, with blond hair and blue eyes. Call on Freya for love, sensuality, prosperity, divination, and any kind of magic. She can also help with the transition and grief that comes with death.

Hecate

The Greek goddess of witches, Hecate once had to assume the form of a cat in order to escape the monster Typhon. Afterward, she extended special treatment to all cats and included them in witchcraft and all things magical. Some think this is how cats came to be known as witches' familiars. Although more often associated with black hounds, Hecate is also depicted along with black cats.

Other than Hecate, there are a few deities who either transformed into the shape of a cat or held the cat as a sacred companion. Ceridwen, the Welsh goddess of wisdom and mother of the famous bard Taliesin, was accompanied by white cats who carried out her orders. The Norse goddess Hel, on the other hand, was aided by black cats.

The Mayan jaguar god of the underworld manifested as a jaguar and was also seen as the night sun that travels from west to east in the underworld at night until it rises again in the daytime in the lands up above.

Ovinnik

An ancient Polish god, Ovinnik appeared as a black cat and was called "the spirit of the barn." He was worshipped among farmers and known for watching over domestic animals and chasing away evil ghosts and troublesome fairies.

Call on him for protection from malicious spirits or to watch over your cats, dogs, and gerbils (or whatever).

Ra

Ra himself sometimes appeared as a huge cat, and in this form he was referred to as Maau. He is mentioned as the "Great Cat who is in Heliopolis" in the Egyptian Book of the Dead. During a solar eclipse it was thought that Ra, as the Great Cat, fought and triumphed over Apep, the god of darkness, who took the form of a giant snake.

Call on Ra to help you win your battles, no matter what they might be.

Sekhmet

Unlike the milder and loving Bast, Sekhmet was called "the lion-headed" and depicted accordingly. Also called "the Terrible One" or "the Powerful One," Sekhmet was the goddess of war—and, ironically, healing (I suppose that was convenient). She was depicted with the head of a lioness, black skin, and flaming eyes. Sometimes said to be the daughter of Ra, the sun god, Sekhmet was also a solar deity.

If you need a fierce defender or ally, you can call on Sekhmet. Work with her for protection for you, your home, or your loved ones.

Magic the Cat

Working with a god or goddess can be very rewarding. Cats, of course, do such things without effort, which is possibly why witches find them so useful to have around. It can be a little bit more difficult for humans, but I'm sure you can manage. Remember to always be respectful, say please and thank you, and don't expect them to do miracles on your behalf unless you are willing to put in some of the work yourself (and maybe not even then—sometimes the gods know something isn't a good idea, even if you don't). It doesn't hurt to bring them presents, either. Deborah often puts flowers on the altar, or food, or a pretty crystal. Personally, I think a nice mouse would go over well, but I have never been able to convince her of that.

● ● ●

If you wish to work with a cat deity, here are a few spells you might find useful.

Spell for Finding Your Own Deity

Sometimes it is obvious which god or goddess we are supposed to be working with—either we are instantly drawn to them or they make themselves known in one way or another. If you are constantly seeing owls, for instance, perhaps they are signs from Athena. But if you can't figure out who to call on for a particular issue or you want to explore a new relationship with deity and can't figure out which one, try doing this spell. This is designed specifically for cat-related deities, but you can easily broaden its reach by changing out some of the names.

Spell components: A cat deity statue or statues (ones of Bast are easy to find) or pictures of cat deities (you can print these off the internet or open a book to a page that shows them), a white or silver candle, a sage smudge stick or cleansing incense of your choice (lemon, orange, or lavender). Optional: if you are doing the spell outside under a full moon, you can use a hand mirror or a dark bowl full of water to look into after you have recited the spell.

Set up your images of deity. Cleanse your energy with the sage or incense by wafting it around you as you visualize yourself becoming clear and open. Light the candle and say the spell, then sit for a while in silence to see if you get a flash of intuition or guidance. If using the mirror or bowl of water, gaze into it and see if a glimmer of deity appears.

Bastet so kind, hear my plea
Send a sign of deity
Sekhmet fierce and Ra so bright
Guide me to the god who's right
Freya, Hecate, witches' queens
Help me see what can't be seen
Spirits wild and spirits free
Show me the god who's right for me.

Spell for Asking a Deity for Help

If you are having a tough time with something and need to ask one of these cat gods or goddesses for help, you might want to set up an altar that is specific to that deity (an Egyptian cat statue for Bast, for instance) or anything that might appeal to a cat-centric god, such as cat toys, catnip, or some treats. The full moon is a particularly good night to call on a cat deity, although you can always do so whenever you have the need. Depending on the deity, you may want to use a specific candle color, such as black for Bast and red for Sekhmet.

Blessed one, fierce and feline
Come to me in this time of need
Spring to my aid with your grace and power
Slink to my side with subtlety and passion
(Name of deity), I call you
(Name of deity), I call you
And ask for your help and wisdom
O blessed one, fierce and feline!

A Cat Deity Meditation

If you want to connect with a particular deity or take turns connecting with more than one, you can try doing this meditation. It might help to have a picture of the deity to gaze at before starting.

On the night of a full or new moon, or at noon on a sunny day, light a white candle. If you want, you can burn sage or any incense that puts you into a calm and meditative state. You can also play soft music in the background; I like to use CDs with nature sounds or lightly chiming bells.

Of course, if you can get your cat to sit with you while you do the meditation, all the better.

Start by making yourself comfortable. After all, no cat would ever consider doing a meditation without having a comfy cushion or seat to sit on! Light the incense, start the music, and then light the candle.

Close your eyes and picture the deity you wish to connect with. If you are doing the meditation at night, think of the moon (whichever phase it is in) and envision the deity stalking through the night in their cat form. If it is daytime, see the deity as a cat curled up contentedly in a sunny patch outside or across the room.

Imagine reaching out with your hands and your spirit to feel the strength, contentment, and wisdom of the god reaching back toward you. Sit quietly for a while and see what happens. Be sure to thank the deity when you are ready to end the meditation.

Cats

CHARLES BAUDELAIRE (TRANS. CYRIL SCOTT)

All ardent lovers and all sages prize,
—As ripening years incline upon their brows—
The mild and mighty cats—pride of the house—
That like unto them are indolent, stern and wise.

The friends of Learning and of Ecstasy,
They search for silence and the horrors of gloom;
The devil had used them for his steeds of Doom,
Could he alone have bent their pride to slavery.

When musing, they display those outlines chaste,
Of the great sphinxes—stretched o'er the sandy waste,
That seem to slumber deep in a dream without end:

From out their loins a fountainous furnace flies,
And grains of sparkling gold, as fine as sand,
Bestar the mystic pupils of their eyes.

CHAPTER 4

Cat Naming & Finding a New Cat

*There are few things in life
that are as heartwarming than
to be welcomed by a cat.*

• • • • • •
TAY HOHOFF

41

•   •   •

Cats come to us in various ways. Sometimes we plan to get one, like the time I looked on Petfinder.com with the intention of adding a fourth cat to the household in honor of one I lost. Sometimes they surprise you, like the time I went to the shelter to get that fourth cat (Angus, as it turned out) and came home with two instead of one. I swear, it wasn't my fault. I had every intention of getting just one. I even went back three times, trying to decide which one to take: the adorable fox-faced yellow boy cat I went there for or the small and sweet calico who shared his room along with about twenty other cats.

Finally, I went back one last time and sat in the middle of the floor. I said, "Okay, gods, whichever one of these cats sits on my lap, that's the one I'm taking home." Angus, the shy yellow boy, came and sat on my lap and purred like a maniac. "Okay," I said. Then he got up, and the tiny girl cat—a stray who they thought was three or four, who had been there for a year—came and sat on my lap in his place. Not one of the other cats in the room so much as looked in my direction. I could practically hear the gods laughing.

And yet, I wouldn't have given up Samhain (she was black and orange, what would you have named her?) for anything. Like I said, sometimes you have a plan and sometimes the gods have one for you. Not to mention what the cats have in mind…

Naming a Cat

You have to be careful what you name a cat. If you don't believe me, here is a cautionary tale from my own life. When I was a college student, I got the most adorable kitten in the whole world. Seriously—this kitten was so endearing, the only names I could come up with for her were horribly cutesy (and I am not the cutesy type). So I thought I would be clever and ironic and named her "Killer."

Oh, boy. She turned out to suit that name all too well. Not that she was purposely violent. On the contrary, she was obsessively loving, to the point where every time I came home, she would race across the apartment and up my leg, clinging on with the tiniest, sharpest claws of any cat I've ever had. Adorable, yes, but before long I was covered with scratches from head to toe.

So take my word for it: you want to be careful what you name a cat.

On the other hand, many cats turn out to suit their names in much more positive ways. For instance, my black cat Magic is the first true familiar I've ever had. Did I know that when I named her? Maybe on some level; it is hard to say. Lots of cat names don't seem to carry that much weight with them (her brother Mystic isn't all that mystical, and their mom, Minerva, was certainly a goddess in my heart, but timid and sweet in general), but that doesn't mean you don't want to choose the perfect name for each cat.

If you listen well enough, some cats will tell you their names. And there are those who believe that the name you call a cat by doesn't matter because they all have secret names we humans will never know, unless they happen to whisper them in our ears as we sleep.

Of course, as witches, we can also ask. You can start by spending some time with any new cat who joins your household to get an idea of their personality and see if you can get a sense for who they are. Try out a few names and see if they seem to fit and if the cat responds or instead gives you that look—the one that says, "What on earth were you thinking?" I almost named Magic and Mystic "Onyx" and "Agate" for their black and gray colors (and the fact that I make gemstone jewelry), but when I tried using those names, I just got indignant sniffs and raised kitten tails as they strolled away. Your new cat will probably let you know, too.

Spell for Discovering Your Cat's Name

If the previous idea doesn't work and the name doesn't come to you, you can always try doing a spell to discover exactly the right name for your new companion. Try doing this spell right before bed and see if the name comes to you in a dream. Or take a piece of paper and a pen and write down whatever pops into your head. If the cat will sit near you while you're saying the spell, even better, but it should work anyway.

Spell components: A white candle, a bit of the cat's fur, and either a list of possible names you have written out by hand or a book of names. I like *Llewellyn's Complete Book of Names: For Pagans, Witches, Wiccans, Druids, Heathens, Mages, Shamans, and Independent Thinkers of All Sorts* (K. M. Sheard, Llewellyn, 2011).

Light the candle, place the fur on the book or list, and say the spell.

> *A cat needs a name like a witch needs a cat*
> *Perfect and fitting and right*
> *A name for the daylight without a disguise*
> *A name for the shadows of night*
> *Help me to see this cat's proper name*
> *The one that will fit like a glove*
> *Let it ring in my ears and appear in my head*
> *To suit this new cat that I love.*

Keep in mind that a cat may have more than one name. In her book *Catspells: A Collection of Enchantments for You and Your Feline Companion*, Claire Nahmad suggests that all cats have three names: a pet name or folk name for the cat's "child-spirit," a "name of distinction," and a magical name. She also has some suggestions for suitable cat names that are worth checking out. Also check out Ellen Dugan's book *The Enchanted Cat* for her cat name suggestions.

Female Cat Names

ABATHA: the Good Witch of the East from *The Wizard of Oz*

AGATHA: "goodly"—a witch name back in the day

AINE: a legendary swan maiden, also a Celtic goddess; good for a cat who is graceful and dignified

AMBER: like the gemstone/resin of the same name, golden or orange, sacred to Freya

ANGELICA: "angelic"—especially appropriate for a very well-behaved cat or one who seems to be especially connected to the spirit world

ASTARTE: a witch goddess

AURELIA: "golden"—perfect for yellow or buff-colored cats

AURORA: goddess of the dawn, fitting for a brightly colored, energetic cat

BAST: the Egyptian goddess, often symbolized by a black cat statue; good for regal or Egyptian-looking cats

BIANCA: "white"—perfect for white cats

BRIDGET: "strength"—also the powerful Celtic goddess of healing and creativity

CRYSTAL: a good name for a cat who is attracted to stones or magical work, or who has a sparkling personality

DIANA: "goddess"—a good name for a witchy and mysterious cat

FREYA: the Norse goddess of love, also associated with cats; a good name for a very loving or powerful cat

HECATE: the Greek and Celtic goddess of witches; perfect for a black cat

GRISELDA: "battle maiden"—good for a feisty cat or one who defends the household

JASMINE: "enchantment of the night"—good for a cat that is mostly active at night or drawn to flowers, especially if they are on your altar

LUNA: "moon"—a Roman goddess of the moon and also another name for the moon itself; perfect for a white or yellow cat

MINERVA: after the goddess or Minerva McGonagall, the powerful teacher in Harry Potter who transformed herself into a silver tabby cat

MORGANA: another witchy goddess

Onyx: the black stone is highly protective, and the name is good for black cats or any who are very protective of their people (this name works for male cats too)

Phoebe: another moon goddess; good for cats who are mysterious

Selene: "moon"—goddess of the full moon; good for a light-colored or serene cat

Sibyl: "wisewoman"—for the cat who seems to commune with the unseen

Titania: the faerie queen from Shakespeare's play *A Midsummer Night's Dream*; a good name for a haughty and regal cat

Male Cat Names

Ambrose: "immortal"—the wizard Merlin was also called Ambrose, so this is a very magical name

Arthur: "bear"—King Arthur is the most famous to have this name, which makes it a good one for a regal or powerful cat

Bagheera: after the cunning black panther in Rudyard Kipling's *The Jungle Book*; perfect for a clever black cat who is loyal and strong

Binx: the black cat in the movie *Hocus Pocus*

Caradoc: "love" or "beloved"—an ancient Celtic name good for a powerful and very loving cat

Ebony: for a black cat

GREYMALKIN OR GRIMALKIN: a traditional witchy cat name; Nostradamus had a cat named Grimalkin (this name also works for female cats)

GRIMOIRE: a witch's Book of Shadows is a grimoire and one of our most prized magical tools; this is a good name for a cat who seems to know things

JET: like the powerful witch's stone (actually a resin), a good name for a black cat

LEO: "lionhearted"—a good name for a brave and powerful tawny-colored cat

LLEWELLYN: "like a lion"—associated with magic because of the many books put out by the publishing company of the same name, this Welsh name may also be associated with the god Llew

LYNX: like the wildcat who bears this name; good for a sleek and stealthy cat

MERLIN: the most famous magician in mythology; perfect for a mysterious and magical cat

MIDNIGHT: a popular name for both male and female black cats

PAN: a playful god of the fields and music; good for a cat who seems to always be in good spirits and full of energy

PYEWACKET: the Siamese cat familiar in the movie *Bell, Book, and Candle*; a good name for a magical Siamese

SHADOW: black or gray cats who follow you around
  might like this name

SPHINX: the cat-headed Egyptian statue; perfect for silent
  and mysterious guardians of the household

THOTH: the Egyptian god of magic and the moon; would
  suit any magical and powerful cat

TIGER: good for a cat who is convinced he is wild and
  ferocious

A few cats with interesting names who belonged to famous
people:

MARK TWAIN: Beelzebub, Blatherskite, Buffalo Bill,
  Apollinaris, Sin, Sour Mash, Tammany, Zoroaster

YOKO ONO: Charo, Misha, Sascha

T. S. ELIOT: (who wrote *Old Possum's Book of Practical
  Cats*, which is famous for talking about the names
  of cats and is the basis of the play *Cats*) Noilly Prat,
  Pattipaws, Tantomile, and Wiscus

So let's face it, you can pretty much name a cat anything
you want. If you look at the names of my cats, you can see that
these days I like to use names that have some kind of magical
or mystical bent: Magic, Mystic, Minerva, Angus Mac, Luna,
Samhain, and so on. But I have also used names out of favorite
books: Shadowspawn was a black cat named after a character
in a fantasy novel who was a cunning and mysterious thief, and

Askelon came from that same book, where he was a demigod of sleep. I gave him that name because as a kitten, he always slept right by my head and helped me to sleep.

Even before I discovered I was a witch, I used the names of gods, like my black cats Lares and Penates, who were named after gods or spirits who are guardians of the household. Of course, we thought when we named them that they were boy cats, and they turned out to be girls (it's a long story), but the names still suited them.

In truth, you can name your cat anything you like, as long as the cat agrees.

Getting a New Cat

Let's start at the beginning: getting a new cat. Sometimes the cat finds you. I once had a cat show up in my driveway in the middle of the night in February. The poor thing had feet that were bloody from the cold ground, and she had clearly been living rough for some time. I thought maybe she was feral (a cat that is essentially wild) and caught her with a Havaheart trap so I could get her spayed, checked out, and then adopted. As I sat with her in my mudroom, waiting for a friend to pick her up and take her to a spay/neuter clinic, she started purring as I talked to her, even as scared and battered as she was.

Needless to say, she didn't go out for adoption, and when the cat I named Melisande died suddenly six months later of renal failure, even my normally pragmatic vet said to me, "I believe this cat came to you so she would have a safe and comfortable place to die after six months of finally being loved." I think Dr. B. was right, and as heartbreaking as it was, I was happy the gods had sent me this cat so I could do just that. It wasn't the purpose I would have chosen, but it was a good one, nonetheless.

Thankfully, I've had a lot of stories with happier endings, or at least much longer tales. Many of the most wonderful cats I've had have been happy accidents, or at least not what I thought I was looking for when I went in search of a new cat. For instance, there was that time I went looking for one kitten and came home with two kittens and their sickly, terrified, completely unadoptable mom. Those kittens were Magic and Mystic, and their mom, Minerva, ended up being a wonderful cat, even if it did take her two years before she was willing to trust me, and hardly anyone besides me ever saw her. Taking this family home was one of the best "not what I planned" things I've ever done.

The lesson here, I suppose, is to keep an open mind and pay attention to the signs when the universe sends you an unexpected gift of a cat.

Spell for Finding a New Cat

If, however, you are ready to make room for a new feline in your home and you want to make sure you find the one who is just right for you, you can also try using this spell.

Spell components: A couple of bowls, one filled with water and the other either with cat food or, if you would rather use something you can eat later, a can of tuna or something else a cat would like—maybe a catnip mouse or a small toy.

If you happen to have a statue of Bast or a cat figurine, place that on your altar, a table, or a floor mat along with the bowls and toys. Light a white candle to symbolize the beacon you wish to guide your new cat to you and you to them. Say the following with an open heart:

God and Goddess, send to me
The perfect feline company
A cat to feed and love and hold
A kitten tender or adult bold
Send the cat who'll suit me best
And stand alone from all the rest
Help me find the cat that's mine
With a guidance that's divine
Here, kitty kitty
Here, kitty kitty
Here, kitty kitty
I call you home!

You can also find cats that need homes in various other places. Sometimes my local PetSmart has cats from the nearby shelter in cages near the front of the store. There are also often ads on Craigslist or in the newspaper. My vet's office has a board where people can post pictures of cats that need good homes, including ones who have been found or ones where the owners can no longer keep them. Some neighborhoods have feral cats, and I have had a number of friends who have put in the hard work of taming a few or catching the kittens when they are young and still able to be socialized.

If you have your heart set on a particular breed, you still might find one in a shelter or through a rescue organization. I once wanted a kitten of a particular silvery-gray color and was able to find one at a farm a few towns over because the people posted a note about barn kittens at my vet's.

There are so many cats that will never find homes and either spend their lives in shelters, are put to sleep, or roam the streets until they meet a terrible death. Please spay or neuter any cat you do adopt so you don't add to the problem (plus you won't have to listen to a female cat yowling when she is in heat or put up with spraying or fighting in a male). Also, I hope that you will never, ever consider declawing a cat just to save wear and tear on your furniture. Many people aren't aware that when cats are declawed, they actually have the first joint of their toes cut off. (My vets won't even do it, bless them.)

A NOTE FROM

Magic the Cat

*I*f you are looking for a new addition to your home, please consider adopting from your local shelter. Unless you have your heart set on a certain breed (and even then, you might be able to find one in a shelter), there is no reason to buy a cat. There are thousands of kitties that need to find a good home, many of them living in shelters for years before the right person comes along. And don't just look at the cute kittens. Yes, I was an adorable kitten when Deborah found me and my overly large brother, but she also took our wonderful mama, who was kind of on the skittish side and probably wouldn't have found another home. Older cats and special needs cats can be very rewarding and would probably spend the rest of their lives living at a shelter (if they're fortunate enough to be in a no-kill facility). Believe it or not, black cats are adopted less than any other color, due to old superstitions about us being unlucky. Ridiculous! Black cats are the best, especially if you're a witch.

The Kitten and the Falling Leaves

WILLIAM WORDSWORTH

That way look, my Infant, lo!
What a pretty baby-show!
See the Kitten on the wall,
Sporting with the leaves that fall,
Withered leaves—one—two—and three—
From the lofty elder-tree!
Through the calm and frosty air
Of this morning bright and fair,
Eddying round and round they sink
Softly, slowly: one might think,
From the motions that are made,
Every little leaf conveyed
Sylph or Faery hither tending,—
To this lower world descending,
Each invisible and mute,
In his wavering parachute.

But the Kitten, how she starts,
Crouches, stretches, paws, and darts!

First at one, and then its fellow
Just as light and just as yellow;
There are many now—now one—
Now they stop and there are none.
What intenseness of desire
In her upward eye of fire!
With a tiger-leap half-way
Now she meets the coming prey,
Lets it go as fast, and then
Has it in her power again:
Now she works with three or four,
Like an Indian conjurer;
Quick as he in feats of art,
Far beyond in joy of heart.
Were her antics played in the eye
Of a thousand standers-by,
Clapping hands with shout and stare,
What would little Tabby care
For the plaudits of the crowd?
Over happy to be proud,
Over wealthy in the treasure
Of her own exceeding pleasure!

CHAPTER 5

Living with Cats

I had been told that the training
procedure with cats was difficult. It's not.
Mine had me trained in two days.

• • • • •
BILL DANA

• • •

There are many rewards to living with a cat, but sharing your home with a feline is not without its challenges. (Of course, your cats may think that about living with you, too.) This chapter isn't a how-to manual as much as it is a practical and magical aid to surviving and thriving with your cat companion—and vice versa, naturally.

Cats are wonderful creatures, but like people, some of them are easier to get along with than others or have more restful personalities. Some cats have, shall we say, challenging traits that can be difficult to live with over time. They may have bad habits, not play well with others, or just generally be stubborn. (A cat stubborn? Imagine that. *MAGIC THE CAT, I'm looking at you.*) Tortoiseshell cats are actually quite renowned for their "tortie-tude," as I discovered with a cat named Luna who simply refused to entertain the idea that she wouldn't get her own way.

Behavior and Misbehavior

If you have a cat who is causing disruptions and difficulties, there are many different ways to cope, including behavior modification (check out books by Jackson Galaxy, among others), products like Feliway (a cat pheromone), and talking to your vet. But while you are looking for practical solutions, you can also try doing this spell for a tranquil household.

Spell for a Tranquil Household

This is a good spell to do during the dark moon, although it can be performed whenever you need it. If you can get the cat to sit with you as you do the spell, that's great. If not—and let's face it, if the cat was cooperative, you probably wouldn't need this spell—the personal items will suffice.

Spell components: A white or light blue candle, a bit of the problem cat's fur or something to symbolize that cat (like a food dish or collar or a picture), and, if you have one, a calming stone such as rose quartz or lapis (otherwise, use some salt to represent earth). You can burn some lavender incense or dab a bit of lavender essential oil on the candle. Fill a dark bowl with water.

Place the candle behind the bowl of water, where its light will fall on the surface, and light it and the incense, if using. Sprinkle a bit of the water on the cat's fur (or whatever you're using) and say this spell:

> *Calm as the water*
> *Soft as the air*
> *Bring peace to this household*
> *And all those who share*
> *Strong like the earth*
> *Bright like the fire*
> *Send calm and tranquility*
> *As I desire*
> *Smooth ruffled fur*
> *Mend bad behavior*
> *Let tranquility reign*
> *For all here to savor.*

Spell to Integrate a New Cat

If unrest arises as you try to integrate a new cat, you can do a variation on this spell, aimed in particular at helping your new and existing kitties to get along and adjust to the change in circumstances.

Calm as the water
Soft as the air
Bring peace to this household
And all those who share
Strong like the earth
Bright like the fire
Send calm and tranquility
As I desire
Smooth ruffled fur
Let good friendships start
Help the old accept the new
Into our family's heart.

Cats always know whether people like or dislike them. They do not always care enough to do anything about it.

WINIFRED CARRIERE

Magic the Cat

Keep in mind that it can be difficult for cats to share their territory with a stranger. And yes, you are part of that territory. Take things slowly and be patient. If you can, allow the new cat to stay separate for a while and give the existing kitty or kitties time to get used to the new smells. Be sure to give your current cat lots of extra attention and love so they don't feel neglected or replaced. And don't listen to the people who say it is okay to just let the cats fight it out until they establish the pecking order. Not only can that lead to injuries and expensive vet bills, it establishes a dangerous precedent. Yelling doesn't help either. Do some research on cat behavior, allow the cats to take things at their own speed, and make sure that everyone has a safe place to retreat to—including you—when the yowling starts.

• • •

Very few cats are good all the time. That's part of their charm. (No, really—Magic the Cat told me so.) The truth is, even most dogs aren't well-behaved all the time, and they're a lot easier to train than most cats. My cats are nearly perfect (no, really— Magic the Cat told me so), but even they have their moments. When Magic was younger, before she developed arthritis and it got difficult for her to jump to high spots, she had a regrettable tendency to jump on the counter in the kitchen when I was preparing dinner.

She didn't consider this to be a problem. As far as I could tell, she knew that there was a "no cats on the counter" rule; she simply didn't believe it applied to her. The other cats might get up on the counter, but as soon as they knew I'd spotted them, they'd jump right down. Not Magic. I'd be cutting up some chicken or something and she'd leap onto the counter six inches away. When I said, "Hey! You're not supposed to be up there! I'm right here," she'd just give me that haughty Egyptian stare, as if to say, "Uh-huh. And your point?"

Of course, she was also smart enough that when I pointed to the floor and said, "GET. DOWN," she'd get—at her own speed, of course, just to prove she'd intended to do it all along.

In this particular case, it is a little hard to say who was training whom. But for the most part, I was able to keep the cats off of the counters the majority of the time, as long as I wasn't foolish enough to leave anything particularly tempting up there. If you are struggling to establish good behavior patterns in your cat or cats, there are a few basic rules to follow. One is to be clear about the rules. Every time a cat got on the counter, the cat was told to get off. They never got fed up there, and there was sometimes a squirt bottle aimed in their general direction. (After the first few times, I rarely had to actually use it. They knew what a water bottle meant.) Consistency is important. If you only apply the rules some of the time, the cat can't be expected to learn what is and isn't allowed.

Stay calm and try not to get angry, even if the cat just shredded your favorite curtains. Don't take it personally. The cat is being a cat, which is not to say they might not have shredded the curtains on purpose because you did something that upset them, but they're animals, not people, and they are acting on instinct. If you want a bad behavior to stop, you need to figure out what is motivating it and react accordingly. Cats have pretty basic motivations most of the time: anger, fear, hunger, curiosity, boredom, frustration. If you can figure out what is causing the behavior, you are more likely to be able to come up with a solution.

In Magic's case, for instance, she wasn't really jumping up on the counter because she wanted the food. She liked to supervise and wanted to see what I was doing. She often insisted on sitting on my shoulder while I cooked, just so she could watch. So I got a stool she could sit on and learned to let her sniff at the ingredients. Usually she'd get bored after a while and wander off. Like I said, hard to say who was training whom, but at least she wasn't getting on the counter anymore.

Spell for Good Behavior

Once you have taken all the practical measures you can to work toward good behavior, you can also try this spell to encourage it.

If your cat will sit near you for this spell, it is great to include him or her. Otherwise, simply light a white candle and envision your cat behaving perfectly. This is a good one to do under a full moon, although it can be done anytime it is needed.

Spell components: A piece of tiger's-eye stone and a small bell. If you happen to have a statue of Bast, you can also put that in front of you.

Light the candle. Hold the stone in one hand. Ring the bell once at the start of the spell.

Dear cat, please behave
Well and not badly
Stay out of trouble
And those places forbidden
No fighting or growling
Peeing only where proper
No hissing or howling
No breaking or shredding
Dear cat who I love
Please try to behave
And I will be grateful
Sincerely, your slave.

Ring bell again and snuff out the candle. Put the stone on your altar or wherever the cat is having the most issues.

Cats and Training

Contrary to popular belief, cats are actually quite trainable if you have patience and are willing to use basic behavior modification techniques. Cats even have been trained to pee in the toilet and flush afterward, although I've never been that ambitious with mine. In general, cats are smart and will learn many things on their own. For instance, my cat Mystic (who is huge) would stand on his hind legs with one paw on either side of the bedroom doorknob. He clearly knew that was how you opened the door, although he couldn't get enough of a grip to be able to make the knob turn, thank goodness.

When I was trying to get little Luna to behave (a task which turned out to be impossible because she really wanted to be an only cat), I worked with a clicker and treats to teach her some simple tricks. She would jump up on a stool and sit, for instance, in order to get a treat, and then jump back down to the floor and sit again on command. She learned it so fast, I only had to use the clicker a couple of times, and then I simply said, "Up, Luna," and "Sit."

Luna was actually a very interesting case (if you weren't living through it). She had all sorts of bad behaviors in the year and a half I had her, few of which I was able to train out of her. When I finally had to concede that she needed to live in a different place, and found her a new home that was what she wanted—no other cats and a whole house to run around in at will, instead of being stuck up in a room most of the time so she wouldn't either chase or be chased by the other cats—almost all of those behaviors disappeared.

I couldn't believe it when her new mama told me she never jumped up on the counter and threw things on the floor, something she did on a regular basis at my house. In this situation, the answer was to change her entire surroundings, which is pretty drastic. (Thankfully, I was able to find her the perfect new home, and I get to visit her every couple of weeks. There was a lot of praying involved, let me tell you.)

Luckily, most cats can be trained to do most reasonable things and sometimes some fun extras as well. Mystic's trick was to jump up for treats and catch them in mid-air between both paws. Magic will play fetch, if she's in the mood. Both those things took a little practice and some patience on my part, but the cats wanted to do them, which is half the battle.

There are many things a cat will do instinctively, like use a litter box (their mamas teach them, but even without that, you can give them a box and show them how to scratch in it, and they usually get the idea). Both Magic and Mystic's "tricks" were based on their instinctual knowledge of how to catch (and play with) prey. If you can find ways to train a cat that work with their own inclinations, you will find things go much easier.

Many cats, like Luna, will also learn to do things if you reward them. Luna is very food-oriented, so she would do almost anything for treats. Some cats are just as happy with attention and praise. If you can figure out what motivates your cat, that really helps.

Whether you are trying to train a cat to stop doing something bad or start doing something fun, it will require patience and a certain insight into your own cat. There are also lots of good books out there, although what works with one cat might not work with another.

Spell to Ease Training

While you're following all the practical advice, you can also try doing this spell to make things go more smoothly.

Spell components: Any books you happen to have on training cats or cat behavior (if you don't have any, you can write down some names of ones you might want to use—see the back of the book for a few recommendations), some treats in a bowl, a cat toy, a small bowl of water, and a blue or white candle. If your cat will sit with you, that's great. If not, you can either use a picture of the cat you want to train or keep his or her image in your mind.

Light the candle. While holding the toy, visualize going through the motions of training the cat, and then visualize the cat successfully doing whatever it is you want him or her to do (or not do). Put the toy down on the altar or your lap, then say the spell.

I ask the universe to help me train this cat
To do what is right and not what's destructive
Let me be lovingly patient during the process
So we end up with results that are constructive
(hold up the treats)
Help the cat respond well to praises and treats
So our work together is entertaining
(flick a little water with your fingers)
Let the cat respond well to soft-hearted scolding
So we succeed together at training
So mote it be!

Snuff out candle, and feed the treats to the cat.

> **Cats seem to go on the principle**
> **that it never does any harm**
> **to ask for what you want.**
>
> **JOSEPH WOOD KRUTCH**

A Cat in Motion

There are few things in a cat owner's life that are more traumatic than having a lost cat. I've had a number of cats disappear on me over the years (although none since I started keeping mine indoors, which was part of why I did it). Some of them eventually came back, usually skinnier and a little the worse for wear. Some never did, and it broke my heart and kept me up at night wondering what had happened to them.

If one of your cats gets lost, do the practical things—call the local shelters and vets (people often notify those folks if they see a stray cat hanging around, even if they don't try to catch the cat and bring it in), put up signs, and maybe call the local radio station (ours puts out public service announcements about lost cats). If you're on social media, you can also post a picture of the cat there.

Then while you're waiting, you can do this spell, which is mostly a prayer.

Spell to Find a Lost Cat

Spell components: A picture of the lost cat (if you have one), a bit of the cat's fur (if you can find some in a brush or on the floor or furniture), a piece of paper cut into the shape of a heart, a pen, and a white candle. Optional: a picture or statue of Bast.

Place the supplies in front of you on an altar or table, then light the white candle. On the piece of paper, draw a picture of a house (it doesn't have to be anything fancy, so don't worry if you're not an artist) with a figure to represent you next to it, then write the cat's name inside the house. Place the picture and fur on top of the paper, and say the spell. You can substitute the name of another god or goddess for Bast if there is one you follow.

> *Let this light guide (cat's name) back to me*
> *Let them hear my heart's call and return home*
> *Safe and sound, sound and safe*
> *Bast, goddess of cats, watch over mine*
> *And send them back to me soon*
> *Let this light guide (cat's name) back to me now*
> *So mote it be!*

Leave the candle burning in a firesafe container until you need to put it out. Repeat every day until the cat comes home or it becomes clear he or she probably won't.

Spell to Find a Perfect Cat Sitter

Some cats are easy to leave behind when you travel. There was a time when I had five cats that all went in and out, ate the same food, could be depended on *not* to eat everything I set out for them on the first day, and got along well without me. Back in those days, all I needed was for a friend to stop by every couple of days and check to make sure everything was okay and that there was still food and water in their bowls. Easy peasy.

Things are considerably more complicated now. I have fewer cats but they all eat in separate rooms, with different food measured out twice a day. They don't go outside, so the litterboxes have to be cleaned daily, and one of them is sick and on medicine. For a while I was able to get by with having a friend visit in the morning and the evening. Because of the sick kitty (and serious pouting on Magic's part when I'm away for more than three days, to the point where she stops eating), I now have someone actually come and stay at the house.

The cats are much happier, and I feel less guilt about going away to writing conferences and such. I also know that if there is a medical emergency, my cat sitter will be able to take the kitty to my vet, who will just bill me later. I still call every couple of days to check in, but it has worked out very well.

You may not need to go to these lengths, but if you are going away for longer than a day or two, or if you have cats with special needs, you may have to get a cat sitter (whether they stay at the house or merely visit once or twice a day). Obviously, it is good to get recommendations from your friends or your vet, but if you are still searching, you can try doing this spell to help you find exactly the right person to take care of your babies.

Spell components: place a few of your cat's possessions, like food and water bowls and a toy or two, in front of a phone book (or, if you are new-school, your cell phone). Light a white or blue candle and say the following:

> *Help me find the perfect one*
> *To watch my cats when I'm away*
> *To keep them fed and keep them safe*
> *To watch them sleep and watch them play*
> *Dependable and right on time*
> *Someone kind who has the knack*
> *To take my place until I come back.*

Spell for Safe and Easy Cat Travel

Even trickier than traveling without your cats is traveling *with* them. Although some cats are perfectly fine hitting the road—I know someone whose family always took their cat on summer vacation in their RV—most cats don't take kindly to being removed from their homes and will let you know this loudly and often.

Plus, of course, you have to be certain you can keep them safe. I am strongly in favor of keeping a cat restrained in a carrier while traveling in a car, no matter how much the cat protests or how unfair you think it is. For one thing, if you are in an accident, the cat can be thrown around the inside of the vehicle, and even if they aren't seriously injured, if someone opens the door, they will probably run off.

I also had a friend who was traveling across country (from her old home to her new home) and allowed her cat to roam around the car. When she stopped, the cat got out the window, which was only opened a crack to let in air. Needless to say, she searched and searched, but the cat was never found. My friend never forgave herself, and it broke her heart.

This is not to say you can't take your cat with you when you move or go on a trip. A fellow author introduced me to her kitty at a convention we were attending, which was a few hours' drive from where she lived. The kitty had medical issues and wouldn't take her medication from anyone else. Thankfully, the hotel we were staying in allowed pets for a small additional charge, so the kitty, when I met her, was happily ensconced in a room with her own litter box, her own food, and a nice big bed to lie on. The only precaution my author pal took was to make sure that maid service didn't come in. The cat seemed perfectly content. (And I got a kitty fix when I was far from my own babies.)

I don't suggest taking a cat along on trips unless you have to or unless the kitty is one of those rare animals who actually likes to travel. But if you don't have any choice, make sure you keep the cat as safe as possible, give him or her some smells from home, medicate if necessary (some cats need to be given tranquilizers, in which case it is always a good idea to try it out ahead of time since they don't all react well to these medicines). For an added layer of protection, do this spell before your trip.

Spell components: If using a cat carrier, you can actually put it on or near your altar or inside your magical circle. You will also need one of your cat's toys or some bedding, a picture of the cat or some fur or the cat itself (if it is willing), a small bowl with some catnip and some treats, plus a small plate, some salt and water, and either a sprig of rosemary, dried rosemary, or some rosemary essential oil.

If using the carrier, place the toys, bedding, and bowl of catnip on top or right in front of it. Otherwise, simply use a table or the floor. Sprinkle the catnip over the toys, bedding, and carrier. Place some on the plate and sprinkle it with salt and water, then add the rosemary. Add a treat or two, keeping them away from the other items on the plate, and then say the spell.

> *Great Goddess who watches over the wild and the tame*
> *Keep watch over my cat as we travel together*
> *Help my cat to be comfortable and unafraid*
> *Keep my cat safe from harm and trauma*
> *Let us travel easily until we reach the end of our journey*
> *And make the trip as trouble-free as possible*
> *So mote it be!*

Now give the cat the treats.

Spell to Ease the Stress of a Move

Moving is tough on everyone—lots of change and commotion, plus the inevitable stress. But cats find change particularly unsettling, especially when that change involves their territory. Hey, they spent all that time marking it. And you probably didn't ask them if they wanted to move. (Hint: They would have said no.)

There are a few things you can do to try making a move less upsetting. Make sure that the cat is safe during the process and can't get loose. Establish a space in the new house where the cat will feel comfortable, preferably one that has toys and furniture from the old home. Give the kitty extra love and attention if you can (I know, you'll probably be frazzled too); they need to know that even if everything else has changed, you are still there.

And if you have an outdoor cat, wait at least a few weeks, more if possible, before letting the kitty outside. If the cat hasn't bonded to its new home, there is a very good possibility it will set out in search of the old one, no matter how far away it is. I had a cat years ago that ran away from the apartment I moved to, back to my old house. It was across town and took her months, but she eventually found her way home. Thankfully safely, although she was in pretty rough shape by the time she got there. I had other cats who disappeared after moves and never did show up again. It was heartbreaking.

To prevent or ease stress, you can also try this spell.

Spell components: A bit of the cat's fur, a few toys or a piece of cat furniture (a favorite pillow will do), a picture of the old house and the new house (if you have them; if not, you can write the addresses down on two pieces of paper and place them next to each other), and a green or brown candle. If the cat will sit with you for this, that's great, but it's not necessary.

Light the candle. Hold the cat's fur in your hand and say:

> *Home is where the heart is,*
> *but my heart is wherever you are, (name of cat).*

Move the toys or pillow from in front of the old house to the front of the new house.

> *Your heart and home are safe with me.*
> *Come with me, my friend, and we will*
> *play and love in new places.*

Put the fur in front of the new house.

> *We will travel together in joy, and I will do my best*
> *to create a wonderful new home for us.*
> *Let go of the old and travel with me to the new.*
> *Look, we have a fun new space to explore!*

Close your eyes and visualize the cat safe and happy in its new environment, then snuff out the candle.

In or Out

When I was growing up, all our cats were inside/outside cats who roamed outside at will. So when I had my own cats, I followed that practice too, at least until I moved to the place I live now. At my little farmhouse in the country, there are all kinds of predators, including coyotes, foxes, and large hawks, not to mention the crazy people who drive fifty miles an hour down the narrow road in front of my house.

When I first moved in, I had two elderly cats, one of whom was dying of cancer. It was an easy decision to keep them inside. Then when I got Minerva and her kittens, I decided to try having indoor cats. I'd always kind of felt that it was unfair to restrict my cats to the indoors, but I was getting to the point where my nerves simply weren't up to dealing with cats that came home beaten up or didn't come home at all. I figured that if they hated it, I could always change my mind. Plus, of course, the average life span for an indoor cat is twelve to fifteen years, and that of an outdoor cat is six to seven.

To my surprise, they weren't miserable at all. Minerva, who was the only one who had ever gone outside (Magic and Mystic were born in the shelter), was happy to sit in a window. Who could blame her? The last time she'd gone outside, she'd gotten pregnant and her people took her to a shelter. The kittens seemed perfectly content.

My vet bills went down, and I didn't have to jump every time I heard a strange noise or the sound of a car. As a bonus, I got to have bird feeders for the first time in my life. My vet, incidentally, is a huge fan of indoor cats. She says they live longer and have less issues (including no fleas or ticks). And when they do have issues, you can rule out all sorts of possibilities right away.

Spell for the Protection of Cats Who Go Outside

Whether or not you let your cats outside is a personal decision. I'm not going to try persuading you that just because that's what I decided was right for me and my cats, it is right for everyone. But I will say that I can't imagine ever having an outdoor cat again. Neither my nerves nor my wallet are up to it. If you do allow your cats to roam, as I did for years, you might want to do this spell for an extra bit of protection. (But if your cat comes home smelling of skunk, don't blame me.)

Spell components: A bit of your cat's fur, a shed claw or an imprint of their paw (you can do this with water on a piece of paper—you don't have to be able to see it, just have the essence of it), a piece of paper, a black candle, and a piece of black ribbon, thread, or yarn. You will also need a small amount of salt in a bowl and a sage smudge stick or any protective incense, such as rosemary.

Write the cat's name on the paper. If you're using an imprint of the kitty's paw, put it on that same paper. Place the fur and the claw or paw print in the middle of the paper. Light the candle, place the ribbon in a circle around the fur and claw or paw print, and sprinkle salt over the ribbon. Waft the smoke from the smudge stick or incense around the circle as you say the spell.

> *Keep this cat safe from harm*
> *And when he wanders far and wide*
> *With this magic and this charm*
> *Protect this cat while he's outside.*

Crazy Cat Person Cure

I don't know about you, but I'd have a dozen cats if I could— maybe more if I had the space, the time, and the money, which I don't. For many years I had five, which probably moved me pretty close to crazy cat lady status (some would say I was firmly there). But the truth was, I did have enough space and time and love for all those cats, and nearly enough money, although I stuck with that number for many years because I knew it was my limit. Mostly I aim for three when the universe doesn't interfere.

Only you can judge how many cats is your magic number. The temptation is always there to add just one more, especially when you see a cute kitten or hear about a cat in need. And certainly, if you have the room, taking in just one more can change a cat's life forever. But if you don't have the space or your existing cats are unlikely to adjust well or your lease says "one more cat and you're *out*," one way to channel all that cat love is to volunteer at a shelter. That way you get to help a lot of cats without having them all live under your roof. Shelters almost always need people to help clean, socialize the cats, or assist at adoption events.

If you don't have a convenient shelter nearby or can't spare the time (or, like me, know you would end up bringing home half the animals anyway), you can always donate to local or national cat organizations or help out in other ways.

Spell to Not Become a Crazy Cat Person (aka volunteering without adopting)

When you are yearning for more cats but can't have them for whatever reason, try doing this spell. You don't need anything to go with it, although you can put up a picture of your existing cat or cats and light a white candle.

> *Take the love I have for cats*
> *And help me share it wisely*
> *Only taking on the number I can truly care for*
> *And finding ways for me to channel*
> *The love I have that goes beyond*
> *So that I and my cats can thrive together*
> *In peace and without longing for more*
> *So mote it be!*

St. Jerome's Cat
Traditional English Nursery Rhyme

St. Jerome in his study kept a great big cat,
it's always in his pictures, with its feet upon the mat.
Did he give it milk to drink, in a little dish?
When it came to Fridays, did he give it fish?
If I lost my little cat, I'd be sad without it;
I should ask St. Jerome what to do about it.

I should ask St. Jerome, just because of that,
for he's the only saint I know who kept a kitty cat.

CHAPTER 6

Cat Health

*The problem with cats is that they get
the exact same look on their face whether
they see a moth or an axe-murderer.*

• • • • • • • • • •
PAULA POUNDSTONE

85

• • •

In a perfect world, all of our cats would live long, healthy lives and die in their sleep of old age at about twenty-five. They'd never get sick or injured, and we'd never have to pay for expensive vet bills. Wouldn't that be nice?

The reality, of course, is that just like us, some cats are healthier than others. Some have genetic or age-related issues or get into accidents or fights with other cats (or critters if they go outside). I have had four different cats over the years who had one type of cancer or another—like people, if they live long enough, usually something goes wrong.

I have also had plenty of cats who lived long and remarkably trouble-free lives, so you never know. My oldest was nineteen, and despite being a feral barn cat when I got her and going outside almost her entire life, she had virtually no health issues until right before she died. On the other hand, there was Samhain, who was three or four when I adopted her from the shelter (she was a stray so they didn't know for sure) and who was diagnosed with chronic renal failure two years later at an unusually young age for such things. She lived six more years, which was remarkable, but it just goes to show that you never know.

When you take a cat into your home, you are making a commitment to care for it in sickness and in health, which can mean a substantial outlay in time and money. This is something to be considered when deciding whether to get a cat or add one to an existing household. Even a healthy kitty requires basic care, such as vaccinations, the occasional vet visit, food, litter, and flea treatments for those who go outside. (Plus treats, toys, cat furniture, and all the rest.)

Of course, we all hope that our cats will stay healthy and strong. There are some things we can do to make that more likely—yearly vet visits can catch problems early (that was when Samhain's CRF was diagnosed because she had lost a substantial amount of weight—if we hadn't caught it then, she probably would have died much sooner than she did), and vaccines can prevent others (I lost a cat years ago to feline leukemia and it was hellish; if your cats go outside, please get this vaccine on top of the usual ones).

Keeping them inside prevents them from getting hit by cars or attacked by wild animals or dogs or getting into fights with other cats. Getting your cat spayed or neutered as soon as they are old enough not only makes them less likely to spray in the house, go wandering, and get into trouble, it also prevents yet more unwanted kittens from being added to the multiple thousands born every year that don't find homes.

Even indoor cats are at risk from simple things that might be found around the home, like cleaning fluids or plants that are poisonous to them. A piece of tinsel off the Christmas tree, if swallowed, can get wound around a cat's intestines and kill him; the same goes for otherwise innocuous items like dental floss or yarn. Just as you would baby-proof a house for a new child, it is a good idea to walk through your home with an eye to what kind of trouble a cat can get into. Make sure that anything dangerous is tucked away safely in a cupboard or up too high for the cat to get at it.

And once you have done all the practical things, it can't hurt to toss in a spell for continued good health, just in case.

Spell for Cat Health

Spell components: A blue candle on a firesafe plate or flat holder; a statue or picture of Hecate, Bast, or Sekhmet; some fresh or dried healing herbs (calendula, rosemary, lemon balm, and lavender are good choices); a picture of your cat or a small amount of fur; and something pointed to write on the candle with (toothpicks work well). Do this one under the full moon if you can. Optional: a piece of tiger's-eye or lapis.

Place the picture of your cat or the fur in front of the representation of the goddess. Carve the cat's name into the candle and place it to the right of the picture, putting the stone to the left if you are using one. Light the candle and sprinkle the herbs over the cat's picture, then say the following:

> *Great Goddess, she who watches over cats*
> *Watch over mine and keep them healthy*
> *Let them be strong and able*
> *Keep illness and trouble far away*
> *And let them live to a comfortable old age*
> *With your love and blessing*
> *Great Goddess, she who watches over cats*
> *Watch over mine and keep them healthy.*

This spell can be done for multiple cats at one time. Simply carve all their names into the candle and use pictures or fur from each one.

Spell for Cat Healing

Sometimes, no matter what we do, something goes wrong. Whether it is an illness, an accident, or a fluke, it is hard to watch our beloved cats deal with bad health. (Mystic once had a tooth break off at the gum line and had to have surgery to remove the rest so it wouldn't get infected.) No spell is a substitute for good professional care, but as witches, we know it can't hurt to ask for some extra help from our own experts.

For this, you can call on Bast or Sekhmet the lion-hearted if there is a real fight for the kitty's recovery. You can also call on Hecate, especially if your cat is black. You could also invoke Bridget for her healing skills.

Spell components: A statue or picture of Bast (or whichever goddess you are calling on), a blue or white candle on a fire-safe plate (you can use black if you are banishing illness), a picture of your cat or some fur plus a whisker if you can find one (check the bed or couch where the cat usually lies), a small pointed tool like a toothpick (the tip of your athame will work too), healing essential oils (rosemary, calendula, lemon balm, lavender) or dried herbs if you don't have oils, one of the cat's toys or some catnip, a bell, and a sage smudge stick. If possible, a tiger's-eye, lapis, or bloodstone. (When our cats are ill or injured, sometimes the last thing we want to do is hunt down a bunch of spell ingredients. If you are too upset or the situation is urgent, you can always simply say the spell and hold the cat in your mind and heart.)

Carve the cat's name into the candle and dab it with the essential oil while visualizing the cat when they were healthy and happy. If using dried herbs, rub them up and down the sides of the candle or sprinkle onto the plate the candle will be sitting on. Place the stone in front of the statue or picture of the goddess as a gift. Put the fur/whisker on the plate holding the candle and sage both it and the cat's picture using the smudge wand, visualizing the illness or injury being wafted away along with any fear or stress the animal might be experiencing.

Light the candle and hold the toy or catnip in one hand, then say the spell:

> *Goddess wise and Goddess kind*
> *Heal the cat that's on my mind*
> *Strengthen all they need to fight*
> *Heal by day, heal by night*
> *Heal by night, heal by day*
> *Until they're well enough to play*
> *(toss the toy up and down or sprinkle the catnip*
> *on the plate with the candle and ring the bell)*
> *So mote it be*
> *So mote it be*
> *So mote it be!*
> *(ring bell again)*

A NOTE FROM

Magic the Cat

*B*eing sick is no fun for a cat. We can't tell you where it hurts or let you know we're nauseous without drastic measures, like throwing up in your shoe. (I personally have found that one quite effective.) We depend on our people to take care of us, but usually we're so freaked out that we aren't as cooperative as we might be when we are feeling better. Please be patient with us, and try not to take the hissing, growling, and occasional impulsive smack with a paw personally. Deep down, we really appreciate it. I promise.

Spell for a Vet Visit to Go Well

Whether a cat is healthy and going in for a checkup or dealing with an ongoing issue or a crisis, going to the vet is often upsetting and traumatic for both you and the cat. Some cats are perfectly content to hop into their carriers and take a ride to see the nice vet. If you have cats like this, I hope you appreciate them!

My cats are more normal, meaning that they fight going into the carrier at home. I have been known to spend twenty minutes chasing Angus around the house because he psychically knew I was going to try putting him in the carrier right that very minute, even though it had been out for days. I'm not sure which one of us was more traumatized. (Okay, it was him, but I was a close second.) Magic and Mystic will even sleep in the carrier if I put it out early…right up until the point when I actually want them to be in it.

Then, when you get them to the vet, they often resist coming out of the carrier. Mystic was so impossible to get out without hurting him that I finally had to buy one that also opened from the top so we didn't have to dismantle it every single time. Plus, of course, there is the yowling in the car the entire way there.

And all of that is before the vet even starts the exam or gets out a needle or that thermometer. (Poor kitty.) This is a simple spell that can be said the night before a vet visit or as you're getting ready to go. If you are doing it the night before, you can light a white candle. Otherwise, don't bother since you're just as likely to forget and leave the candle burning in the rush of capturing the cat and getting out the door!

> *God and Goddess, hear my plea*
> *Help this go well for my cat and for me*
> *Let the vet be kind and wise*
> *No bad news, no pricy surprise*
> *Keep my cat as calm as you can*
> *Until we're home and safe again.*

Spell for Protection from Pests

If you have cats who go outdoors, you are going to have to worry about pests: fleas, ticks, worms, all sorts of disgusting little parasites that can be both annoying and a danger to your cat's health. (And to yours, if they bring them inside.) I have to admit, one of the best side effects of not allowing my cats outside is no longer having to fight those wretched fleas! (Although Angus did once bring them home from the vet's and then kindly spread them to all the other cats.)

There are plenty of treatments for pests these days, and prevention is definitely the best way to go. Fleas and ticks have developed immunity to some of the treatments that have been around for a while, so make sure you check with your vet to see what the newest, best thing is. Cats with health issues may not be able to tolerate the more potent (and effective) treatments; Samhain was already battling renal failure during the time Angus brought home the fleas, so I ended up using a flea comb on her until the outbreak was over.

Either way, it is a lot easier to prevent pests than it is to get rid of them. So after you've done all the usual practical steps, try adding this spell for an extra layer of protection.

Spell components: A symbol of pest prevention (this can be a flea comb, the tube or box from a flea treatment, worm medicine, or anything else you have on hand), a picture of whichever pests you want to prevent (you can draw a rough sketch yourself or print one off the computer) with a large black X drawn across it, a black candle, and a bit of your cat's fur (optional).

Place everything in front of the candle and light it, then say the spell while visualizing your cat being surrounded by a protective white glow that repels all parasites.

> *No to fleas and no to ticks*
> *No to any little icks*
> *No to pests that creep and crawl*
> *No to nasties one and all*
> *Protect my cat and keep them free*
> *Of all the bugs that bother me!*

Snuff out the candle and pet your cat.

> **The only escape from the miseries of life are music and cats.**
>
> ALBERT SCHWEITZER

Natural Medicine for Cats

Depending on what kind of health issues a cat is facing, there may be natural alternatives to medicines or complementary alternative treatments to go along with whatever your vet prescribes. As always, you will want to double-check with your vet to make sure that nothing you give to your cat will have negative side effects when mixed with their medicines, and be sure that whatever you are using is actually safe for cats—some things that are safe for people, and even dogs, can be deadly in cats.

For instance, there are pain medicines for dogs with arthritis, but there are none that are safe for long-term use in cats. But there are supplements made from glucosamine and chondroitin, the same thing many people take for arthritis. Magic the Cat has been on one of those for a couple of years, and I think it helps. I've read that turmeric can help too, although we haven't tried that. Plus, of course, practical solutions like putting cat stairs by the desk and bed, and an ottoman in front of the couch so it is easier for her to get to places she can no longer jump up to. Heated beds can be comforting for old, sick, or achy cats too. (Don't use regular heating pads; they can be too hot for cats.)

Cats who are constipated might be put on medicine to help them, but you can also add pumpkin to their food, which is rich in fiber. (Some cats like it and some don't.) Believe it or not, cats can also use over-the-counter Miralax, but check with your vet about dosage. For kitties who have to take an antibiotic, acidophilus supplements can help keep them from having digestive upset (this is good advice for people too). But don't use yogurt, since dairy isn't really good for cats.

Cranberry powder or unsweetened juice may help kitties with reoccurring urinary tract infections, if you can get the cat to take it (although special food is what my vet recommends, since she's not a fan of the cranberry approach). Increasing fluid intake helps too. When Mystic and Angus started getting UTIs, my vet suggested that I buy a cat fountain because cats have been shown to drink more water when it comes from a moving source. I was skeptical, but it turned out to be true. Now I have a ceramic cat fountain in the living room and a metal one in the kitchen. (The cheapest ones are plastic, but my experience is that they get pitted and hard to clean.)

Some calming herbs that are safe for cats include catnip (some cats get hyper and some get blissed out, so you will have to see how your cat reacts), valerian, chamomile, and hops. Since Mystic got sick, his favorite toy is an owl stuffed with valerian that a cat-savvy friend gave us. He actually sleeps with his head on it some of the time, like a little tranquilizer pillow. Another good calming soother is Bach Rescue Remedy, which is a flower essence rather than an herb. I use the people version for myself and really swear by it. You will want to get the alcohol-free pet version to give to your cat, though. You can put a couple of drops in her water, directly into her mouth, or even rub it on her ears.

For skittish cats or those with behavior problems, you can try Feliway, which is a product that contains cat pheromones that can calm cats and reduce spraying or inappropriate urinating, fighting with other cats, or simply calm the cat. Some people swear by it. If you like the idea of flower essences, like the Bach brand, cat behaviorist Jackson Galaxy (who has a show on Animal Planet called *My Cat from Hell*) puts out his own brand of essence supplements, including some I tried when I was attempting to integrate Luna into the house. Safe Space, Bully Solution, and Peacemaker were a few that I tried. I do think they helped, although in the end they weren't enough.

If you are going to use herbs with your cats, often just putting them in a pillow or toy will do. Many are safe to ingest in dried form, but don't use essential oils, which are much too strong and could actually kill a cat.

Brewer's yeast added to food may help repel fleas. Don't, however, give them garlic (although I've seen it suggested often, it may be tough to get the dose right enough to be sure it is safe). This is fine for dogs but can lead to anemia in cats when the amounts used are too large.

One of the best treatments for hairballs is a good brushing. Most cats like this and will be happy to be pampered. And don't forget that petting cats is therapeutic for both them and you!

Believe it or not, there are also cat acupuncturists, cat chiropractors, and cat massage therapists. Since all those things help me, I would happily use them on my cats if they were available in my small, rural town. I think it is worth exploring all the options when it comes to keeping your cat healthy.

If you are interested in exploring natural options more extensively, try a book like *The Veterinarians' Guide to Natural Remedies* by Martin Zucker or *The Natural Cat* by Anitra Frazier.

What greater gift than the love of a cat?

CHARLES DICKENS

To Mrs. Reynold's Cat

JOHN KEATS

Cat! who has pass'd thy grand climacteric,
How many mice and rats hast in thy days
Destroy'd? How many tit-bits stolen? Gaze
With those bright languid segments green,
    and prick
Those velvet ears—but prythee do not stick
Thy latent talons in me—and tell me all thy frays,
Of fish and mice, and rats and tender chick;
Nay, look not down, nor lick thy dainty wrists,—
For all the wheezy asthma—and for all
Thy tail's tip is nick'd off—and though the fists
Of many a maid have given thee many a maul,
Still is thy fur as when the lists
In youth thou enter'dst on glass-bottled wall.

CHAPTER 7

Love and Loss

To some blind souls all cats are much alike.
To a cat lover every cat from the beginning of
time has been utterly and amazingly unique.

· · · · · · · ·
JENNY DE VRIES

101

· · ·

I'm going to confess, just between us cat lovers, that this was a difficult chapter to write. There is nothing "theoretical" or "hypothetical" about love and loss for me when it comes to my cats. I've loved many and lost almost all of them eventually, and there is no avoiding the truth: it hurts. On the other hand, I obviously wouldn't keep getting more cats if I didn't believe that every moment of pain was repaid a thousandfold by the joy of having them in my life. For me, at least, the blessing of having a cat far outweighs the inevitable grief at the end, when I have to let them go.

Alas, dealing with the loss of a beloved cat has been the norm for me the last few years. I lost my beautiful calico Samhain three days after Christmas in 2015, after six years of battling chronic renal failure. Her passing was sudden, but I already knew she was losing the battle. When I lost Minerva, Mystic and Magic's mom, a little over a year later, in March of 2016, it was a brutal battle over a couple of months that came out of nowhere. As I write this book in the summer of 2017, Mystic is slowly going downhill—on five medicines and periodic fluids, he is fighting the good fight, but I expect that by the time this book comes out, my big gorgeous gray boy will also be gone, at the age of fifteen, which is quite respectable but not nearly old enough.

If you have ever lost one of your cats, you know that it never gets easier. At best, you can learn to let go with a little more grace, and in the cat's time, not yours. If I have learned anything over the years, it is probably this: not to keep a cat alive for me when he or she is truly ready to move on. It's okay to cry. I do every time, even though I rarely cry over anything else. It's okay to feel as though it isn't fair, that the gods should have given you another day or week or year. I feel that way every single time.

There is nothing I can say in the pages of this book that will make it hurt less. That's the truth, and I won't pretend otherwise. Losing a cat *sucks*. (Yes, that's the technical magical term.) But maybe, just maybe, these spells will help just a little if you have to let go of one of your beloved fur babies. Maybe, like me, you will find some comfort in remembering that the wheel keeps spinning around and will hopefully bring the ones we love back to us eventually, either in this life or another. And once they cross the Rainbow Bridge, they will no longer be in pain or suffering but rather be free to run and play just as they did when they were young and healthy.

I believe that the cats who share our lives are a gift from the gods—a gift so great and wonderful that we only get it for a few too-short years, and therefore we need to appreciate every moment of the time we have with them. When that time comes to an end, I hope you find these spells helpful.

Spell to Ease a Cat's Passing

So, here you are. The moment you have been dreading has arrived, and your treasured companion is reaching the end of the road. If you are like me, you would give anything to make this transition easier for both of you, but especially for your cat.

You can do this as a spell complete with a ritual or, if things are moving quickly, you can simply say it as a prayer.

Spell components: a white candle and a black candle (if you only have two white ones, simply tie a black ribbon or piece of yarn around the bottom of the second one), a pointed implement (such as an athame or a toothpick), rosemary essential oil and a sprig of fresh rosemary (if you don't have the oil, just use the fresh herb), a favorite flower, and a picture of your cat. Optional: a statue of Bast or any deity you follow.

Scratch the cat's name into the white candle and rub it with the rosemary oil or herb. Do the same with the black candle. If you want, you can also draw a heart or the rune sign Gifu (which looks like an X and often stands for a gift) or anything else that has meaning to you. Place the picture of the cat in front of the two candles, and put the flower and the rosemary sprig where you can reach them. If you can have the cat with or near you, that's great but not necessary.

Light the white candle and say:

> *My beloved (cat's name),*
> *you have been a gift and a blessing.*

Place the rosemary in front of the white candle. Say:

> *This rosemary is for remembrance*
> *because I will never forget the joy you have*
> *brought to my life. You will walk with me*
> *all the rest of my days.*

Light the black candle and say:

> *My beloved (cat's name),*
> *the gods gave you to me*
> *and I return you to their loving care.*

Place the flower in front of the candle. Say:

> *There is no true loss where there is love.*
> *I let you go so that you may move on*
> *at the moment you choose.*
> *May the gods ease your passing*
> *as your presence has eased my life.*

Blow out the white candle. Sit with the black candle as long as it feels right or place it someplace safe to burn down.

A Ritual to Let a Cat Go

My circle-sister Chris does this simple ritual to let a cat's spirit (or that of any animal) go after it has passed, especially if she feels as though they are hovering and not quite able to leave.

If you have the cat's ashes or remains, stand near them. Or go outside under the open sky. Light a white candle and speak gently to the newly deceased animal, reassuring them that it is okay to move on. You can use these words or any that seem right to you at the time; repeat as often as necessary.

> *It's okay to go. I love you,*
> *but your time here is done,*
> *and I set you free.*

Just like people, some cats seem to move on completely as soon as they pass, and others linger—sometimes just for a short time, sometimes for years. When Samhain died, I had a clear sense of her presence for a while. (This was not typical for my cats previous to this.)

She died suddenly at home on a Sunday night—probably instantly from a blood clot, which can happen to end-stage renal failure kitties. I was completely bereft and spent most of the night with her near me, her body still curled up in the heated bed (now unplugged) that she loved so much. First thing in the morning, I brought her to my vet, who came in early to deal with this, bless her, and she and my best friend came in and sat with me while I filled out the paperwork to have Samhain cremated.

Now, you have to understand that I have had all my cats cremated—I can't stand to think of them under the ground, although I know lots of people like to bury their kitties—and I have always sent them out for mass cremations, which are much less expensive. I never saw the point of having the ashes since I knew the cat wasn't really there anymore. That had never been a problem until this time.

As I sat there with the paper, my pen hovered over the place to check "mass cremation," but I just couldn't fill in that box. I had the strongest sense that Samhain wanted to come home— wanted it *a lot*. She was just as stubborn in death as she was in life. It didn't make any sense to me, but as soon as I checked the "private cremation" option, I felt much better. Whether it made sense or not, it was very clear to me that this was not just my grief speaking; Samhain was telling me this was what she wanted.

And in fact, when I finally was able to collect the box with her ashes in it a couple of weeks later and place it on my altar, I felt almost at peace for the first time since I'd lost her. It was without a doubt the clearest communication I'd ever had from a cat after death. I felt her presence in the house for months, and I suspect she still checks in occasionally, probably to make sure that I am still doing what she ordered me to.

Cats. They're the boss of me when they're alive and, apparently, occasionally when they're dead.

Spell to Communicate with a Cat Spirit

If you want to try communicating with the spirit of a cat who has passed, you can try the following spell. Don't be upset if it doesn't work the first time you try it or else not in the way you expected it to. After all, cats do what they want, when they want to, no matter what. That's part of what we love about them, right?

Spell components: a picture of your cat, a black candle, a pendulum (if you don't have one, you can make a simple pendulum using a piece of string and a paperclip), and a dark bowl filled with water. If you have a bit of the cat's hair or a whisker, that is helpful, but it isn't necessary. Optional: a few of the cat's favorite treats or toys. This is a good spell to do on a full moon, if possible with the bowl placed where the moonlight can shine on it, whether you are inside or outside.

This spell is designed to give you two different options for communication. If one doesn't work, the other one might. Once you have said the spell, you can gaze into the bowl and see if any images appear (they will likely be faint, and not everyone is good at scrying, so don't worry if this doesn't work for you).

You can also use the pendulum, since let's face it, what cat doesn't like something that dangles? Before you start, test the pendulum to see how it answers since they can vary. Ask a question you know the answer to is yes ("Is my name Deborah?") and see if it swings side to side or in a circular motion. Then ask a question you know is a no answer ("Do I live on the moon?") and it should swing the opposite way; for instance, backward and forward or circling in the opposite direction.

Magic the Cat

Don't forget that cats grieve too. When my mother Minerva died, both my brother Mystic and I were out of sorts and off balance for months. We needed extra love and attention, and patience when we acted out. Plus, of course, lots and lots of treats. Just sayin'. Keep in mind that if you lose one cat, others in the household may be upset by that loss as well, depending on the dynamics between the members of your kitty family. Don't be surprised if the cats who are left seem upset and go looking for the one who is gone. Sometimes if there is only one cat remaining, they get lonely; you might want to consider adopting someone else to keep them company. Personally, I just wanted more treats, so it depends on the cat.

Once you have done the spell, you can sit very still and hold the pendulum out in front of you, held loosely between two fingers. Then you can ask the cat if it is there. If the pendulum moves, you can try asking specific questions (Are you content? Will you come back to me some day in another form?). Just remember that the answers have to be either yes or no.

You will also want to be open to other forms of communication. You may simply sense the cat's presence, or feel as if they have brushed by you, or patted you gently with a paw. Or they could knock over something. Cats, you know.

Quiet your mind as much as possible. Put everything in front of you and light the candle. Then say the spell and try one or both of the methods of communication. You may have to be patient—cats don't always come right away when you call them, do they?

> *(Cat's name), I miss you*
> *(Cat's name), I call you*
> *Come to me if you can, little one*
> *Speak to me in your soft voice*
> *Touch me with your gentle paw*
> *Let me know you're here*
> *(Cat's name), I miss you*
> *(Cat's name), I call you*
> *With love in my heart*
> *I ask you to visit me*
> *Here, kitty kitty*
> *Meow!*

A Meditation for Letting Go of Grief

If there is one thing I have learned from losing those I love—both people and cats—it is that grief is like a living thing. It is different every time, completely unpredictable, and it takes as long as it takes to run its course. Sometimes letting go is easier than you expected. Sometimes it is so gut-wrenching you feel as though you will never be able to take a deep breath again.

And don't let anyone tell you that you aren't allowed to grieve for your beloved fur companion, just as you would for any other friend or member of your family. While we are more attached to some cats than to others, for many of us, our cats are practically an extension of our bodies, and losing them can feel as though someone has cut off one of your limbs—without benefit of anesthesia.

Grief can't be ignored and it can't be hurried...but it also can't be allowed to keep you from moving on with your life, and sometimes we have a hard time letting it go. If you are struggling with this, try doing this meditation. I hope it helps.

Find a quiet spot where you won't be disturbed. You can do this on the night of the full or dark moon or during the middle of a sunny day, whatever feels right to you. If you want, play some music in the background, as long as it is meditative in nature. Optional: Sage yourself before and after with a smudge wand, and rinse your hands and face in a bowl of water. You can also light a white candle and stare at it instead of closing your eyes, if that works better for you.

Sit comfortably. Close your eyes or let them relax as you look at the candle. Take three slow, deep breaths. As you breathe out, picture clouds of gray grief blowing out with each breath. Repeat this a few times until the clouds get lighter in color. Visualize the cat you are mourning, but see them in happier days. Remember how the cat would purr for you, and feel that purr resonate within you, surrounding your heart with the feeling of love.

Send love out to the cat, and then send some inward to yourself, a mental hug as if you were hugging a heartbroken child. Sit for a few moments feeling all that love, then again take three deep breaths and let them out slowly. See your energy growing lighter with every breath. Open your eyes and let out one more long breath, feeling lighter and a little more at peace.

Repeat as often as you need to.

> *No amount of time can erase*
> *the memory of a good cat,*
> *and no amount of masking*
> *tape can ever totally remove*
> *his fur from your couch.*
>
> LEO DWORKEN

My Black Cat

DEBORAH BLAKE

My black cat, mysterious and wise
With glossy fur and gleaming eyes
Soft of paw and rough of tongue
It is for you my songs are sung
My black cat, treasured and true
How I love the things you do
Waking me up at dawn of day
Reminding me how to sleep and play

My black cat, the jewel of my heart
I rue each moment we're apart
And gladly kiss your nose so dear
When once again you reappear
Your purr can soothe my tortured soul
Your presence makes my spirit whole
I bless the gods who sent you here
I love you, cat, from tail to ear!

CHAPTER 8

Connecting with Your Cat

Time spent with cats
is never wasted.

• • • • • • •
SIGMUND FREUD

— 115

• • •

Sometimes when you get a new cat, the connection is instantaneous and goes in both directions. Sometimes, especially with cats who have previous bad experiences with humans, it can be a long, difficult process requiring patience and understanding.

On top of this, of course, all cats have their own personalities and preferences, and you don't always discover what these are until the kitty has come home with you. Even if you knew ahead of time that there are issues, it can be difficult to predict how long it will take to overcome them—if, in fact, they can be overcome at all. Sometimes you simply have to learn to accept certain traits in your cats, such as fearfulness or bossiness (looking at you *again*, Magic the Cat).

When I brought home mama cat Minerva, along with kittens Magic and Mystic, the kittens and I bonded right away. They spent lots of time playing with me or sleeping on me or chewing on me. Minerva, though, was another story. The folks at the shelter thought she might have been abused by her previous owners, and I tend to agree, although there was no way to be sure.

Certainly she was absolutely terrified (of course, being locked in a cage at the shelter for months was probably pretty traumatic too). She never did get comfortable around strangers, and most of the people who came to my house never saw her because she hid in my bedroom whenever anyone other than my closest friends came to visit.

From the very beginning, I let her take things at her own speed. I encouraged her to trust me, but I didn't force it. In fact, it took two years before she would willingly sit on my lap, although I would put her there from time to time and then allow her to run away. Of course, once she decided that my lap was an okay place, she wanted to be there all the time. Eventually she spent every night until the day she died sleeping right up against my hip.

The trick with Minerva was patience and letting her come to things in her own time. In the end, she and I connected very strongly, although she never did connect with anyone else (except her kittens, to whom she was devoted even after they became adults).

Angus, who I adopted a few years later, had been at the shelter since he was seven weeks old. He was seven months old at the time I found him there. The lovely folks at the shelter warned me when I went to meet him that he was shy and wouldn't come anywhere near me. I went into the room he shared with about twenty other cats and sat on the floor.

I didn't approach him, although I did make quiet, encouraging noises. And sure enough, he came right up to me, asked to be petted, and then purred louder than any cat I have ever heard in my life. We sat like that for about ten minutes, until I made a sudden movement of some kind, and *vroom*—he was gone. The shelter people had gotten it wrong; Angus wasn't shy, he was timid. Skittish, in fact, to a slightly insane degree, which he never grew out of, and it's something we're still dealing with over ten years later. (You'd think he would learn I was never going to try to kill him, but no.) Shy is tough. Timid I could deal with, mostly by moving slowly and trying not to startle him.

Much like dealing with people, connecting with cats takes patience, understanding, and a willingness to accept them the way they are. Minerva was never going to stop being afraid; I only had to make a connection deep enough that she was not afraid of me. Angus will always be skittish, so I've had to learn how to connect with him on his terms and not get my feelings hurt by the fact that he occasionally still looks at me like I am Jack the Ripper crossed with the Boogeyman and runs away to hide—at least until the treats come out.

As for Magic the Cat, well, we have one of those special connections, the rare ones that come along only a few times in a lifetime. I love all my cats, but there is no question that I belong to her most of all. Just ask her. That connection just happened, with no effort on my part. If you're lucky, you'll have one of those too, but for all the others that require a little more work, here are a few spells you might find helpful for making the deepest, healthiest, most positive connections with your cats, no matter what their personalities or preferences.

A NOTE FROM

Magic the Cat

*H*ere's the thing about cats: you can't make us do anything. You can ask nicely. You can offer bribes (always good); you can bargain and persuade and beg. But you can't force a cat to love you or like you or even tolerate you if they don't feel like it. What you can do is be kind and patient, and spend some time figuring out why we react to certain things in certain ways. If you can figure out what motivates a cat—whether it is fear or bad experiences, hunger or tiredness, or the desire for affection and attention—you can probably give the cat what it needs to feel safe and satisfied. You'll find it much easier to forge a connection with a cat if you take the time to understand what she is asking you for, and (as long as it is safe and reasonable) give it to her. Now, about that bribe…

Spell to Connect with a New Cat

The first few days, weeks, and months with a new cat are pivotal in establishing the relationship you and this kitty will have for the rest of your time together. This doesn't mean that if things are rough to begin with, they will always stay that way; often it takes a while for cats to adjust to new people and new circumstances. Some, like Minerva, are slow to trust.

Nevertheless, just as you are learning about your new companion in those early days, they are also learning about you. Patience and kindness are of the utmost importance, and just as in any other relationship, clear communication is key. If there are house rules the kitty needs to know, you have to establish them immediately and enforce them gently but consistently.

For instance, if you have a "no cats on the counter or the table" rule, you have to show them that from the moment they come in the door. Don't allow the new cat to walk on the table for a week because you're trying to be nice and then start yelling at her to get down. It will confuse the living daylights out of her. (Also, yelling is bad. All it does is freak them out. And yes, I still yell at mine occasionally, but only in the heat of the moment.)

Be firm and consistent, and, if necessary, reinforce good behavior with treats and attention (different cats are motivated by different things, so one of your jobs in those first days is to figure out what motivates your new cat so you can use that to help with training). But mostly, be loving and give them the space they need to figure out how to feel safe in this new place.

When trying to communicate with a new cat, you may have to go slowly—every cat has their own personality, and while some will become your best friend right from the start, others may be slow to warm up. If that's the case, here is a spell to help you connect with your new cat.

You don't need any props for this spell, although you can always light a white or yellow candle in front of a statue of Bast if you have one. Do the spell in the same room with the cat, even if it won't sit with or near you, and speak slowly and clearly. If you can, make eye contact with the kitty as you say it.

> *Welcome, (name of cat), to your new home*
> *I am your person, and I welcome you in*
> *Know that you're safe here*
> *With love freely given*
> *I can't wait to know you*
> *As you make your inspection*
> *Of all that is new to you*
> *In this place and connection*
> *I promise to care for you*
> *From beginning to end*
> *I hope that you'll like it here*
> *And be my new friend*
> *Welcome, (name of cat), and most blessed be*
> *I am your person—come talk to me!*

Hold out your hand—possibly with some treats—and see if the cat will come sit by you. If so, a few pets at this point are a great thing.

Living with Scaredy-Cats

My yellow cat Angus Mac (named after both the Celtic god Aengus Mac and MacGyver, of television fame, who was a lover and not a fighter) is a scaredy-cat. Don't get me wrong—he's very sweet and affectionate, and if you sit still and let him come to you in his own time, he will reward you with the loudest purr you have ever heard in your life and lots of rubs and head butts. Right up until the moment when you move a tiny bit too fast or, heaven forbid, sneeze. Then he's off so fast, all you'll see is his dust.

Angus is a strange contradiction; he is essentially a happy, cheerful, affectionate cat, but he is also easily freaked out. (Don't even get me started about the four months he had a tough-to-cure eye infection, and I had to put drops and goop into one eye every day. I spent a lot of time trying to look like I wasn't intending to get anywhere near him, and he spent a lot of time sleeping with the good eye open and hiding under furniture.)

Unlike some cats, who are fearful because of something that happened to them, this is apparently just Angus's natural personality. He was brought to the shelter at seven weeks old and lived there until I took him home at seven months old, and it is a lovely shelter, so nobody did anything terrible to him. He was just wired that way.

Minerva, whom I adopted from a different shelter, was also very fearful, but the folks there told me they thought she might have been abused, and after having her for a while, I had to agree. (Apparently the lovely people who owned her brought her to the shelter and said, "This damned cat got pregnant. You take her.")

As I mentioned earlier, it took two entire years before she would sit on my lap, and she never did get comfortable around men. In fact, she hid most of the time people were in my house, other than the few who came often enough that she knew them. People would ask "How many cats do you have?" because I had five, but usually all they saw were Magic and Mystic.

Over time, I was able to conquer Minerva's fearfulness with me and a few of my closest friends, but she never did stop being a generally fearful cat. I did my best to make her comfortable and not put her in situations where she would be afraid, other than unavoidable things like vet visits. She was a gentle and timid cat, and nothing I did was going to change that. Luckily, it mostly wasn't a problem for either of us, but there were times when she was clearly afraid, and I felt awful that there wasn't more I could do. She was one of the main reasons I had to rehome Luna, as much as I loved her, because Luna was so determined to be the dominant cat, she was terrorizing poor Minerva. It just wasn't fair, and there was no way to make it better (believe me, I tried).

If you have a fearful cat, there are a few things you can try beyond the obvious approach of patience and love. Make sure the cat has a place they can go to hide or feel safe. In Minerva's case, it was my bedroom. Angus will hide under the furniture, but some cats prefer to go higher (that's what Samhain did when giant Mystic was chasing her; because she was so light and small, she could jump up to places he couldn't reach).

Jackson Galaxy has an interesting book called *Catification: Designing a Stylish Home for Your Cat (and You!)* co-authored by Kate Benjamin, in which he shows a number of ways to create spaces for the cats in your life. It's worth checking that out, along with some of his flower essence remedies. You can also talk to your vet about medication if the situation is severe. I know people whose cats have responded very well to Prozac (yes, they give it to cats), although the hope is always that it is a temporary solution rather than something the cat will be on forever.

Galaxy and Benjamin go into great detail on how to create just the right kind of environment for your cats, no matter what their special needs might be. For instance, there are cats who like to be up high. Galaxy calls those cats "tree dwellers" and shows you lots of ways to make them comfortable, including cat superhighways—essentially shelves and platforms they can use to travel around the room without ever getting to floor level.

Other cats, he says, are "bush dwellers" who prefer to burrow and hide. Timid or ill cats will often prefer spots where they are underneath couches, tables, or chairs. Angus, when he isn't on top of the highest spot on the cat tree (which is where he goes when he is feeling relaxed), sometimes burrows under the blanket in the bed, so that all you can see is a funny-looking lump in the covers.

It is really important to communicate with fearful cats, although it will probably take a lot more effort than with the easygoing ones. For one thing, as you have probably experienced in your own life, it is hard to listen when you are freaking out. Basically, all you hear is the loud voice inside your own head saying, "Oh no! Oh no! Scary!" It's the same for cats. If you have ever tried approaching a feral cat outside, you will know that it can take days, weeks, or even months to get them to even let you close enough to talk to them.

But you can also communicate through body language. Send them the message that you are safe and nonthreatening by moving slowly, if at all, and keeping your body crouched down so you are less intimidating. Make sure you speak in low, soothing tones, and don't make any sudden moves. Food and treats communicate goodwill, but you may have to put them down and then back away slowly to whatever the cat considers a safe distance.

Spell to Calm a Fearful Cat

Patience is key in communicating with a fearful cat, whether it is a feral cat you are trying to get close to or one of your own cats who has issues. Remember that cats are sensitive to the unspoken, and if you are feeling frustrated or annoyed, they will probably pick up on that. On the bright side, that also means that if you concentrate on sending out feelings of love and acceptance, hopefully they will sense that too.

You can also try doing this spell, which is aimed at calming the cat so communication can flow more smoothly between you. If possible, do the spell with the cat in the room with you, but if you can't do that, you can use a picture (if the cat will sit still long enough for you to take one) or carve the cat's name on the candle you are using.

This spell can also be used to build trust with a feral cat. In that case, you probably won't have a name or a picture, but you can still visualize the cat in your head.

Spell components: A yellow candle for communication (if the cat will be in the room with you, and is prone to sudden moves, make sure the candle is in a safe place, even if it means you can't do the rest of the spell directly in front of it once the candle is lit), a bit of fur or a whisker or a shed claw from the cat if possible—otherwise, you can use their food bowl or something else belonging to them, a small catnip pillow or a catnip toy (valerian will also work, some cats like that as much or more than catnip), a piece of tiger's-eye or rose quartz or crys-

tal quartz, a few cat treats (they make some that are specifically for calming, so if you can find those, they would be perfect).

If you are going to carve the cat's name into the candle, do so. Then put it on your altar or a safe place and put the cat's fur/claw/whisker in front of it. Light the candle, then sit down on a comfortable chair or cushion where the cat might possibly be tempted to sit with you. Put the catnip pillow or toy in front of you and hold the stone in one hand. Have the treats handy. If the cat actually comes to you during the time you are saying the spell, give them the treats (if not, give them later—the energy of the spell will still be clinging to them). Speak in a low, calm voice:

> *Cat of mine, my darling one*
> *Still yourself, be calm*
> *Know that you are in good hands*
> *I'll keep you safe from harm*
> *Hush, my cat, my sweet, my love*
> *There's nothing here to fear*
> *Calm yourself and rest for now*
> *You're safe when I am near.*

Sit for a while and see if the cat will come to you. If the candle is in a safe container, you can leave it burning; otherwise, snuff it out. You can do this spell every day if necessary, or repeat it without the candle whenever you are sitting with the cat.

Spell of Healing for a Cat Who Has Had a Tough Time

Like my Minerva, sometimes you will end up dealing with a cat who has had a difficult time. This could be anything from abuse to illness to the loss of their previous owner. Just like people, cats need time and space to heal from trauma, plus lots and lots of love. You can also try doing this spell for healing.

This is one of those simple spells that is as much a prayer as it is magic. Inscribe a blue or white candle with the cat's name, symbols for healing (such as the Norse rune Uruz), or even the word "healing." If you want, anoint the candle with lavender essential oil or sprinkle some catnip around it. Then light the candle and visualize a glowing white light of healing surrounding the cat before you say the spell.

> *Blessing, little one*
> *Heal, little one*
> *I am here for you, (name of cat)*
> *And send you love and warmth and comfort*
> *I am here for you*
> *Be well!*

Snuff out the candle.

Spell for Mutual Love and Understanding

Not all cats bond with you immediately. If you have a cat that you are struggling to communicate with—or one that is clearly struggling to communicate with you—you can try this spell to ease tensions and facilitate two-way communication, love, and understanding.

Spell components: A small square of cloth and a ribbon or piece of yarn to tie it with (if you have something yellow, that's perfect, but any color will do—natural materials like cotton, wool, or silk are best), some of your cat's fur, a tiny clipping of your own hair, a yellow or white candle on a firesafe plate or in a candleholder, some catnip, either dried lavender or rose petals, and a pointed tool such as an athame or a toothpick. Optional: a small piece of amethyst or rose quartz (a tumbled stone or a couple of chips will do).

Carve your name and the cat's name next to each other on the candle, side by side, and then draw an infinity symbol (like a figure eight turned on its side) around both names to connect them. Place the square of cloth in front of you with the other items nearby. Light the candle.

> *We are in this together, (cat's name)*
> *You and I, separate but striving*
> *Trying to find our way to each other*
> *In heart and mind*
> *Know that I hear you*
> *Know that I love you*
> *Let us be joined in love and understanding*
> *And clear communication.*

Mix your hair and the cat's fur in the middle of the cloth, add the herbs, and the stone if you're using one. Tie the ribbon or string around the cloth to make it into a charm bag, and hold the bag in your hands.)

From now on, it will be easier
From now on, we are not separate
But joined together
In love and understanding
And mutual respect
You are my cat and I am your person
So mote it be!

Let the candle burn for as long as it is safe, and place the bag on your altar or somewhere both you and the cat pass often. If necessary, repeat the spell while holding the charm bag.

Spell to Deal with a Difficult Cat

Cats aren't difficult on purpose. Well, mostly not. They each have their own personalities and their own histories, and not all of them are endearing all the time. This doesn't mean you don't love them, but it can be easy to get frustrated or annoyed with a cat who causes problems repeatedly. Just remember that, like difficult children, difficult cats often need love even more than those for whom it comes easily.

Sometimes cats are difficult because that is simply their nature. In other cases, it is because there are issues with their situation—problems with other cats or not enough attention or any number of other possibilities. Luna was very difficult at my house and is only a little bit problematic (mostly because she is stubborn) at her new home. It also helped that I figured out ways to get her to do what I wanted her to do without having to force her, which only made her push back more.

With any cat whose behavior is outside the norm and causing disruption in the household, it is a good idea to watch to see what triggers it and then see if you can cut down on those triggers.

If you are dealing with a cat that drives you a little crazy at times, this spell can help you to be more patient and understanding…and, if you are lucky, it might even make the cat a bit less difficult. You never know.

Spell components: a picture of the cat, a bit of fur or a cast-off whisker or claw (if you can find one), a light blue or pink candle (for calm and friendship), a piece of tiger's-eye or rose quartz, a catnip toy, and a few treats for the cat plus a cookie or some other treat for yourself.

Place the catnip toy in front of the candle and place the fur, stone, and treats next to it. The fur is to connect the toy to the cat, and the stone and candle are to imbue it with the calming energy. The treats (both yours and the kitty's) are symbolic of the rewards for being less difficult (the cat) and more patient (you).

Light the candle and say the spell in a firm but calm voice. If the cat is in the room, look at them while reciting the spell.

> *Behavior good and temper mild*
> *Goddess, grant my problem child*
> *Patience long and temper sweet*
> *We both earn our favorite treat!*

Sit for a moment and visualize the cat being good and your-self dealing with any issues calmly and evenly. Then eat your cookie. If the cat is there, give the cat the treats. Then hold the catnip toy in your hand as you continue:

Turn disruption into play
And make each day a happy day!

Snuff out the candle and give the catnip toy to the cat. The spell can be repeated without any tools as often as necessary.

Way down deep, we're all
motivated by the same urges. Cats
have the courage to live by them.

JIM DAVIS

A Cat Connection Meditation

If you can do this meditation with your cat in the same room or, better yet, sharing a bed or chair, that's great. Spend a few minutes petting and talking to the cat. But even if you can't, it is still worth doing. I'm pretty sure they hear you thinking about them from two rooms away anyway.

Close your eyes, sit comfortably, and quiet your mind as much as possible. Take long, slow, deep breaths. Think about what it must be like to be a cat and have nothing that needs to be done right this very minute. Sink into relaxation, as if you had nothing more important to do than to sit and drowse in the sun. Visualize yourself as a cat staring into your own cat's eyes. In your imagining, blink your eyes slowly, as cats do. Give a wide yawn. Then reach out a paw to touch your cat. Feel the connection between your eyes, your minds, your hands/paws. Sit with that connection for a while, feeling the love going back and forth between you. Then, when it feels right, open your eyes and give a big cat stretch. Pet your cat or give it some treats, and see if you can feel a difference in the connection between you.

Communicating with cats is difficult but not impossible, despite the fact that most of us don't speak Cat fluently. (Cats, of course, understand English quite well. They just mostly choose to ignore everything we say that doesn't involve food, praise, or otherwise giving them what they want.)

Cats are actually communicating with us all the time. Posture, ear positions, tail movements, and vocalizations all mean something. Some are obvious, like a hiss, which means "stay away." Some are more subtle, like the particular meow that means "I'm in pain" instead of "I'm hungry." If you pay attention to your own cats, you will become attuned to their own particular nuances.

Spend some time observing your cat. When he is relaxed, what does it look like? (Tail wrapped around the body? Eyes partially closed?) What about when she is upset? (Ears back? Fur puffed out? Tail rigid?) If you have a new cat, take the time to figure out what those moods look like and figure out what your cat is communicating throughout the day.

If you're new to having a cat or are dealing with a cat who has issues, you can check out cat behaviorists like Jackson Galaxy or ask your vet for suggestions on the best way to understand what your cat is trying to say. (Here's a hint: if you're in the kitchen and the cat starts meowing loudly, there's a good chance the message is "I want some of whatever you're having.")

Remember that love is a language you and your cat both speak. Take the time to pet or stroke your kitty, talk to them with affection in your voice, give them the occasional treat, and you will probably be rewarded with purrs, head rubs (when they rub their faces on you, it puts their scent on you, which marks you as their person), and snuggles.

> *If there is one spot of sun spilling onto the floor, a cat will find it and soak it up.*
>
> JOAN ASPER MCINTOSH

An Old Russian Prayer

ANONYMOUS

Hear our prayer, Lord, for all animals,
May they be well-fed and well-trained and happy;
Protect them from hunger and fear and suffering;
And, we pray, protect specially, dear Lord,
The little cat who is the companion of our home,
Keep her safe as she goes abroad,
And bring her back to comfort us.

CHAPTER 9

The Cat as Familiar

*I've met many thinkers and many cats, but
the wisdom of the cat is infinitely superior.*

· · · · · · · ·
HIPPOLYTE TAINE

• • •

Not all familiars are cats, nor are all cats familiars, but it is certainly not an uncommon thing for a witch to have a cat who is one. But what exactly is a familiar, and how do you know if one or more of your cats has magical inclinations?

Historically, familiars were thought to be imps or devils in disguise who helped their witch masters to cast evil spells. While some of my cats can be devilish at times, I suspect that most folks these days wouldn't accept this old superstition as fact. (I certainly hope not, anyway.)

There are probably other definitions, but I would consider a familiar to be any animal that has an affinity for magical work and lends their energy to those workings. The best example I can offer is my black cat Magic. (I did mention that you need to be careful what you name a cat, right?)

Until a couple of years ago, I had five cats in my household, but Magic is the only one I would consider my familiar. While occasionally one of the others would show some interest while I was doing something magical (Minerva used to yowl when I recited spells, for instance…maybe she was reciting along with me?), they mostly ignored it.

Magic, on the other hand, always joins me and Blue Moon Circle when we are having a ritual inside. (My cats don't go outside or I'm sure she would happily join us there as well.) We might stand around and chat for a bit in the living room, where our indoor rituals are held, but as soon as we gather around the altar, Magic strolls in from wherever she has been hiding. She walks two or three times around the altar, which is a low, round table, and those standing around it—always clockwise, as is appropriate, as if to tell us we can now begin. Then she either sits underneath the altar (sometimes on my lap, if we are sitting on cushions) or perches on the back of the couch, where she can supervise in comfortable splendor. As soon as we are done, she hops down and strolls back out of the room. We joke that this is how we know the ritual is over, but it is pretty amazing that she does this so consistently. She clearly knows what she is doing. If that's not a familiar, I don't know what is.

I suspect, although I can't know for sure, that there is something about the energy of magic that draws her there. She also helps me when I do energy healing. She will insist—loudly—on getting up on the massage table I use, and then sit on top of my healing client...precisely in whichever area most needs help. She is uncannily accurate in this area as well.

Mind you, my cat Samhain would also do the healing work but never showed any real interest in the magical stuff, so perhaps the energy *is* different and not all cats are attracted to both.

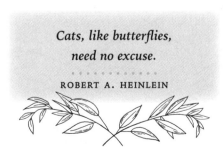

Cats, like butterflies,
need no excuse.

ROBERT A. HEINLEIN

Spell for Finding Your Familiar

Whatever it is that makes a cat a familiar, there is no way to make it happen; a cat either is or is not a familiar. That being said, you can certainly use this spell to ask the gods to help you find a familiar. Once you have done this spell, be sure to pay attention to any cats you happen to come into contact with in case one is the answer to your request.

Spell components: a black candle (white is okay too), some symbol of your magical work (such as an athame or your Book of Shadows), and a picture or statue of a cat.

Light the candle and envision practicing magic with a cat by your side, whatever that means to you. Then say the spell.

> *God and Goddess, hear my plea*
> *Sent the perfect cat for me*
> *One who will my familiar be*
> *And share my magic life with me.*

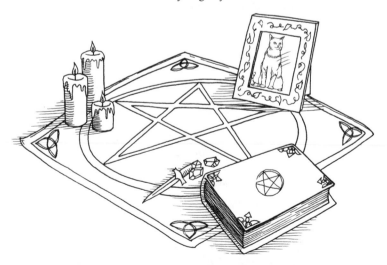

A NOTE FROM

Magic the Cat

*H*aving a cat for a familiar is great. Everyone knows that. But it wouldn't be fair to try forcing one to act as a magical companion if they aren't willing or interested. It is also not a good idea to get a cat specifically because you want a familiar. Unless you are prepared to love and care for an animal whether or not they have any interest in magical work, please don't bring one home. And if you are lucky enough to get a cat who is a familiar, never ask them to do anything dangerous or expose them to herbs or other magical tools that could be poisonous unless you are there to supervise the entire time. Be extra careful with candles and other flames, too. Cats and fire do not mix.

A Simple Cat Blessing

Once you find your familiar, or if you already have one you wish to enhance your magical relationship with, you can do this cat blessing. Light a white or pink candle in a safe place where the cat can't get to it, then say this blessing with your hand or hands on the cat. Note: This blessing can be done for cats who aren't familiars, too.

> *Cat, I bless you*
> *With all my witchy power*
> *With all my loving heart*
> *With the moon up above*
> *And the earth below*
> *I bless you with health*
> *And I bless you with happiness*
> *That you may stay by my side*
> *In magic and joy and harmony*
> *So mote it be!*

A Familiar Ritual to Increase Power

One of the reasons that witches have familiars is because, in theory, it increases their power. If you wish to give your own magical power a boost, you can do this simple ritual with the cat who acts as your familiar.

If you want, you can cast a formal circle by invoking the God and Goddess and calling the four quarters. Otherwise, you can simply set things up on an altar or small table and invite your cat to join you.

Spell components: a quartz crystal, a small bowl of water, a small dish of salt, a sage smudge stick, a red candle, and the cat.

Light the candle and say:

> *With the power of fire, I call on the spirit of this cat,*
> *(name of cat), to increase my power as a witch.*

Hold the crystal for a moment and then let the cat touch it or sniff it. Say:

> *With the power of earth and the energy*
> *of this magical stone, I increase my power as a witch.*

Sprinkle the water lightly over the cat or touch it gently to the cat's nose. Say:

> *With the power of water, I ask that my power*
> *as a witch be as flowing and flexible as this cat.*

Light the sage and waft it carefully over yourself and then the cat (watching for loose embers). Say:

> *With this sacred herb and the power of air,*
> *I declare my intention to work toward*
> *increasing my power as a witch.*
> *I thank the gods for the gift of this familiar*
> *and for the power this cat lends me.*
> *So mote it be!*

Snuff out the sage and the candle and give the kitty lots of affection.

What a Cat Sees:
Auras, Spirits, and More

If you have a cat, you have probably noticed them occasionally looking at something that you can't see. Sometimes, if you get close enough, you might discover something to explain their odd behavior: a small bug or a spot of light on the floor or a scratching sound that hints at a mouse inside a wall. Many times, however, it is clear that they are looking at something, although what that something is, we cannot know.

As mere humans, we can only guess at what they are seeing and how they are seeing it. As witches, we can be pretty sure that cats are sensitive to certain elements that people often can't perceive. Are they watching ghosts or fairies? If they stare at you for a long time when you aren't doing anything interesting, are they looking at your aura? If so, what do they see? The truth is, we just don't know. We can observe their behavior and tell that they are seeing or sensing something that is very obvious to them. I've often thought they must wonder at our lack of perception when we ask, "What the heck are you looking at?"

If you are a particularly sensitive person, you might be able to get some idea of what your cat is seeing, but for the rest of us, this will just continue to be one of the magical mysteries that make cats so wonderful.

Mixing Cats & Magic:
A Few Cautions

As Magic the Cat pointed out earlier, there are certain precautions you will need to take if you are working magic with your feline companion.

Most of the tools we use in witchcraft are perfectly safe—crystals, for instance, shouldn't be a problem unless they are perfectly round, in which case you may find yourself chasing them across the floor. There are, however, a few items that can be problematic and might require special care around your cat.

Herbs in particular can pose a risk for a curious cat. Many herbs are harmless, but it is always a good idea to check before using them in a ritual where your familiar will be present. Keep in mind that just because something is safe for humans doesn't mean it is safe for smaller cats with their more sensitive livers.

Magic the Cat, for instance, has a particular attraction to sage. Thankfully, it isn't harmful, but if I set up the altar table in advance and put the sage smudge stick out with everything else, I will invariably walk back into the room to discover either (a) a cat on the altar table looking completely innocent or (b) gnawed-upon sage leaves scattered all over the table and the floor underneath it. It has actually become a joke in my group, and we've learned to wait until right before the ritual to get the smudge stick out of the cupboard where I store my tools.

Cats are also attracted to some essential oils, like peppermint, which is related to catnip. Even if an herb is safe in a fresh or dried form, the concentrated essential oils can be too much for their sensitive systems, so please use caution. I sometimes use a few drops of essential oil with water in a diffuser, and a cat can get its tongue into that faster than you can imagine. Strong incense may bother their lungs, especially in an unventilated room.

Fire, of course, is a particular danger. If you are using candles around a cat familiar, either make sure that they are too high for the cat to reach, in safe containers, or that you know for certain that your cat will not go anywhere near them. I once had a cat scorch its tail because it was arched over a candle and the kitty apparently didn't feel the heat. It wasn't until I smelled fur burning that I realized there was a problem. (Thankfully, the cat was fine, other than a few singed hairs. My nerves, on the other hand, took weeks to recover.) I wouldn't recommend ever allowing a familiar near an open fire, such as a bonfire.

There are also a few dangers you might not think of, such as string or yarn. We all know that cats are attracted to such things and many times can play with them safely. But thin string or yarn can be swallowed and wind up in their intestines, which can be deadly. Thick ribbon is safer, although don't be surprised if they consider it to be a toy instead of a magical ingredient to whatever spell you're doing.

Note: This is not to say you can't use string, thread, or yarn in your spells—I do it all the time. Just be careful that your cat can't get at them.

A sharp athame can cut your familiar accidentally, although many of them are fairly dull and therefore safe. Dangling sleeves on garb may present a temptation as well. Most of these things are safe most of the time with most cats, so it doesn't mean you can't use them. Just be aware of your own cat's tendencies, like Magic the Cat's sage addiction, and plan accordingly. When in doubt, err on the side of caution, especially if you are working with a new cat you don't know well.

After all, no matter how useful something might be for magical work, I'm sure you'd rather have a safe and healthy cat.

Spell to Keep Your Cat Safe During Magical Work

For an added line of defense, you can do this spell. It is very simple and requires nothing more than a picture of your cat, a white candle, and a white ribbon or piece of yarn. Put the picture of the cat in front of the candle—if you want, you can inscribe the cat's name on the candle. Then circle them both with the ribbon and say the spell. (The full moon is a good time for this one, although the dark moon will also work.)

> *Goddess kind, Goddess wise*
> *Keep this familiar before your eyes*
> *Keep them safe from hurt or harm*
> *As we work our magic's charm*

Items That Might Be Dangerous for Your Familiar

- aloe (the gel is safe, but the outer part of the leaves is dangerous)

- borage

- chamomile (safe in small amounts but can be harmful if a large amount is ingested or if it is consumed over a long period of time)

- comfrey

- eucalyptus

- evening primrose

- foxglove

- garlic (safe in small amounts but toxic in large ones—be very careful)

- holly berries (be careful around the holidays)

- marijuana (can cause seizures and coma, so if you use it, make sure to hide it from the cat)

- mistletoe (be careful if you have this around at Yule)

- pennyroyal (safe as a plant but not when concentrated; do not use for flea treatment)

- tea tree oil (undiluted, it can be poisonous to cats)
- valerian (safe as a plant but dangerous when concentrated into a tincture)
- white willow bark
- wormwood
- tobacco (toxic to cats, so if you use it in Native American medicine work, make sure your familiar doesn't get into it)

This list isn't to suggest that you can't use any of these items. As with anything else, your mileage will vary; some cats get into everything and some will ignore a plate of meat left on the counter. Just use common sense and try to keep anything that might hurt your cat out of reach.

The mathematical probability of a common cat doing exactly as it pleases is the one scientific absolute in the world.

LYNN M. OSBAND

The Cat and the Moon

WILLIAM BUTLER YEATS

The cat went here and there
And the moon spun round like a top,
And the nearest kin of the moon,
The creeping cat, looked up.
Black Minnaloushe stared at the moon,
For, wander and wail as he would,
The pure cold light in the sky
Troubled his animal blood.
Minnaloushe runs in the grass
Lifting his delicate feet.
Do you dance, Minnaloushe, do you dance?
When two close kindred meet.
What better than call a dance?
Maybe the moon may learn,
Tired of that courtly fashion,
A new dance turn.

Minnaloushe creeps through the grass
From moonlit place to place,
The sacred moon overhead
Has taken a new phase.
Does Minnaloushe know that his pupils
Will pass from change to change,
And that from round to crescent,
From crescent to round they range?
Minnaloushe creeps through the grass
Alone, important and wise,
And lifts to the changing moon
His changing eyes.

CHAPTER 10

Power Animals

*In the middle of a world that has always been
a bit mad, the cat walks with confidence.*

● ● ● ● ● ● ● ● ●
ROSANNE AMBERSON

• • •

Regardless of whether or not you have a familiar, you might want to have a feline power animal to call on. Some people believe that they are born with one specific power animal whose job it is to protect and guide them. Others, like me, think that you get different power animals throughout the course of your life, each one particularly suited to helping you deal with whatever issues are challenging you during that particular phase.

You also can have more than one power animal at a time. For instance, you might have an owl for wisdom and a bear for strength. You can call on any animal spirit to help you, but a power animal is more likely to come to you when the time is right and stay with you until you no longer need it.

Power animals, also known as animal allies, are another way of connecting to the spiritual world. Witches are often drawn to animal spirits that have a kind of energy they need, and different power animals are considered to have specific attributes and strengths. This chapter will explore some of the various feline power animals and help you figure out which one or ones might be a good fit for you.

As with all such magical work, the first place to start is by opening yourself to the possibility. Sometimes as soon as you say, "I would like to find a power animal to work with," one comes along. Perhaps, as often seems to happen with cats, the universe is simply waiting for us to open the door. Who knows what might stroll through yours?

You can also ask for a sign to point you in the right direction. If you do the spell for discovering your power animal, for instance, you might then ask to dream of the animal when you go to bed that night. (If so, try tucking a written copy of the spell under your pillow, perhaps with a piece of tiger's-eye.)

Sometimes a power animal will simply show up. If you start seeing crows everywhere all of a sudden—flying overhead, sitting by the side of the road, on television, in artwork, and so on—that is probably a sign that you should be paying attention to that animal. (Of course, in my house, cats will cross your path pretty often, but that's only a sign that I have a lot of cats.) You're not likely to see a tiger sitting by the side of your road, at least in most parts of the world, but you might spot them in posters and ads and movies. Keep your eyes open in case the universe, or the animal itself, is trying to tell you something.

You can also try shamanic journeying. This is a type of trance work that allows you to move through to what is sometimes called "nonordinary reality," or a spiritual dimension that is beyond our ability to sense in the course of our day-to-day lives. By entering an altered state, often through drumming or listening to a drumming recording, you can travel to the spirit worlds, where you can often find and connect with an animal ally. Sometimes shamanic journeys are guided by others, but you can find instructions and online sources that can help you attempt it on your own.

As you take this journey, animals often appear along the way. Sometimes they are simply there to give you a message or provide guidance. Other times one might present itself and make it clear that it is your power animal.

There is nothing wrong with trying to connect with a number of different power animals to see if one of them resonates with you more than the rest. Just remember to keep an open mind and allow the animal to choose you instead of the other way around. After all, you don't want a spirit ally just because you think it is pretty or cool (although I'm sure it will be). You want the one who will be able to help you with your life and with your magic.

Here are some of the more common feline power animals for you to consider. Don't be discouraged if the right one for you doesn't become clear immediately. It might just be that the time isn't right for you to find a power animal this very minute. You can also try the spells that follow.

> *There are people who reshape the world by force or argument, but the cat just lies there, dozing, and the world quietly reshapes itself to suit his comfort and convenience.*
>
> **ALLEN AND IVY DODD**

Bobcat

Bobcats are a small wildcat with a short tail, tufted ears, and funky fans of facial fur. Unlike its lynx cousins, it is only found in North America. It tends to be solitary, so as a power animal it may be a sign that it is time to take a step back from the world for a while. It could also be a comfort during a time when you are feeling alone or help you to make peace with your own solitary nature or circumstances. It is also associated with patience, awareness, cunning, and the inner self.

Cheetah

The cheetah is the fastest animal on earth (on land, anyway). They are tan with black spots and have a tuft on the end of their tails. Like any superior athlete, they are long, lean, and built for speed. As a power animal, the cheetah says, "No more standing still. It is time to move!" It may be helpful to connect with the cheetah at times of rapid change or when you need things in your life to pick up speed.

Cheetahs were an important part of Egyptian culture. They were a symbol for royalty, and there was a goddess named Mafdet who had the head of a cheetah and fought against evil and those who perpetuated it. If you feel as though you are under attack, try asking a cheetah power animal for help.

Domestic Cat

Although not as exotic as the rest of their wild cousins, the house cat can also be a power animal. Anyone who has lived with a cat knows that they can be mysterious, powerful, beautiful, enchanting, mischievous, affectionate, protective, entertaining, loving, and sometimes outright magical. What more could you ask for in a power animal? Some people believe that their own beloved cats stay around after death and watch over them. Domestic cats are good power animals for independence, cleverness, and all forms of magical work.

Leopard

The leopard is a large, dangerous cat with black spots on yellow or gold. They are excellent hunters, silent and deadly, but also beautiful and full of confidence and grace. If you are in need of more of either of those, or if you need to get in touch with your own personal power, the leopard may be a good power animal for you. But don't expect it to be particularly gentle with its lessons—if it tells you something, it would be in your best interest to listen.

*After dark
all cats are leopards.*

Lion

The lion has sometimes been called "the king of beasts." It is regal and powerful. It is also very much family oriented, and if the lion spirit comes into your life, it may be time to focus on family or any other close-knit group, raising children, or situations that require working as a team. The lion is often associated with the sun, perhaps because of the tawny circle of mane that is such a distinctive feature on the male. It is the symbol for the Egyptian goddess Sekhmet, as well as Mithra, a Persian god of light. The lion may bring more light to your life or help you to feel powerful and capable of achieving anything. It may also be a sign that it is time to use your strength to help others.

Lynx

The lynx (usually thought of as the larger version of the bobcat, although the bobcat is, in fact, a member of the lynx family) has tufted ears, a ruff, and large padded paws. They come in four main varieties, including the smaller bobcat, and unlike the bobcat, can be found in Europe and Asia, as well as North America and Canada. It has adapted to a variety of climates, from the temperate to the snowy. According to Native American traditions, the lynx as a power animal is associated with secrets, arcane knowledge, and magical information. It can be especially useful if you are working with clairvoyance or seeking to delve deeper into the psychic arts.

Mountain Lion

Also known as a cougar or puma, the mountain lion is a graceful and powerful animal. They symbolize courage, power, leadership, strength, and silence. The mountain lion may help you to hone your abilities in any of these areas. They may come to you at a time when you are facing challenges that involve leading others or finding the balance and strength in your own power. Known for their silence and patience, they can also help you to find an inner stillness when you need it the most.

Panther

The panther is a magnificent member of the cat family. The name can be used to refer to either jaguars (found in South and Central America) or leopards (found in Africa and Asia). There are also Florida panthers, which are actually a subspecies of cougar. But when most of us think of panthers, we think of the gorgeous and powerful black panther (which can be either a leopard or a jaguar). Black panthers have long been associated with the mystical and were sacred to both the Aztecs and the Mayans.

Unlike most cats, panthers are comfortable with water. They also climb trees and are often pictured lazing regally on a large branch, high up off the ground. The panther is fierce, powerful, cunning, and at home in any environment. It is a good power animal to work with if you need to learn to adapt more easily or become comfortable in difficult situations. The panther can help you to master your own mystical abilities and tap into your personal power.

Tiger

Like the panther, the tiger is also fierce and strong. Also like the panther, tigers like the water and will swim for pleasure. They are especially valued in India and China, and are the national animal of Bangladesh, India, Malaysia, and South Korea. The largest of all the cats, their distinctive stripes and powerful physiques have made them the focus of many cultures, but unfortunately they are now an endangered species.

The tiger is one of the twelve animals in the Chinese zodiac and considered to be a symbol of the element of earth, as well as power, energy, protection, royalty, and generosity. The Hindu goddess Durga was often pictured riding on the back of a tigress. If a tiger shows up as your power animal, it may be time to use your strength and energy to their fullest or take advantage of whatever adventures or opportunities lie before you.

A cat is a lion in a jungle of small bushes.

Spell for Discovering Your Power Animal

If you feel as though you might have a power animal but haven't been able to figure out which one is right for you, try doing this spell to lead you to your magical match.

Spell components: pictures of any wildcat you think might be your power animal (print these out from the internet or get a book out of the library, if you don't happen to have one with them in it already; if you don't want to do either of those, you can always do a rough sketch of each animal and put the name of the animal underneath—don't worry if it isn't great art, as long as you know what each one represents; if there are one or two animals you are particularly drawn to, statues or figurines are great too), a dark bowl filled with water or a scrying mirror, a small bag or sachet filled with lavender, a brown or green candle, and a sage smudge stick. Optional: a drumming CD to play in the background.

Place the pictures or statues of the animals in front of the candle. Place the bowl of water or mirror to one side and the sachet to the other. Light the sage and waft it over yourself from your feet to your head, cleansing yourself of daily stresses and worries and leaving yourself open for any messages that might come. If you want, you can leave the sage smoldering in a firesafe dish.

Light the candle and spend a minute thinking about what it is you would want a power animal to bring to your life. Do you need protection? Guidance? A psychic boost? Different power animals have different gifts, so making it clear to the universe what you are looking for in one might help to clarify which animal is right for you. (Of course, one might have chosen you already, knowing that it is what you truly need.)

When the time feels right, say the spell.

> *I ask the universe to send a sign*
> *A message from the gods divine*
> *I seek my perfect animal of power*
> *In this day and in this hour*
> *I seek the one who matches me*
> *A strong companion, wild and free*
> *Send me a sign so I will know*
> *And to me now my animal show!*

An animal may pop into your head right away or one of the pictures in front of you might call to you. If not, look in the bowl or mirror and see if any images appear. If you are still not getting anything definite, take the lavender sachet and place it under your pillow, then ask the gods to send your power animal to you in a dream.

Don't be discouraged if nothing happens right away. Like any other cats, power animal felines can't be rushed. Keep your eyes open in the days and weeks to come for any other signs or indications of a particular animal.

Spell for Connecting with
Your Power Animal Attributes

Many times we are given a power animal that has attributes we lack or need more of, such as courage, strength, or wisdom. If you want to connect more strongly with those particular attributes, you can do this spell. This one is best done under a full moon.

This is a fairly simple spell, as much a prayer as anything else. If you have a picture or statue of your power animal, you can use it as a focus. Otherwise, just light a white candle once the moon has risen and say the spell from your heart.

God and Goddess, this I ask
That you grant me those traits
That my power animal has in abundance
The ones that I need
The ones that I want
The ones that I lack
Please grant me _____
(list the attributes you hope to attain)
And help me to use those abilities wisely
And to the best of my abilities
So mote it be!

Magic the Cat

*A*s any cat will tell you, there is very little difference between the domestic cat who sits on your couch and the wildcats who roam the forests. The domestic ones are just better at letting people wait on them hand and foot. So-called tame cats share many of the same characteristics with their wild cousins: they are fierce hunters, sleek and graceful, silent and stealthy, and capable of adapting to almost any circumstances—unless they don't want to, in which case they can become as feral as any cougar or lynx. But because of this strong connection, you can always ask your feline familiar, if you have one, to assist you in working with a feline power animal.

A Blessing for a Power Talisman Using Tiger's-Eye

Sometimes it is good to have a talisman to carry around that reminds us of our power animal's presence. You can look for a charm or amulet in the form of your animal, of course, and hang it around your neck or on your keychain. Or you can create this simple talisman from a piece of tiger's-eye, which will work for any feline power animal.

Spell components: Salt, water, a brown or green candle, a sage smudge stick or the incense of your choice or a feather, a candle to represent the gods (black is good if you follow Bast or Hecate, otherwise white is fine), plus the piece of tiger's-eye you are using. A small tumbled stone is good if you are going to be carrying it in your pocket or purse or tucking it under your pillow. If you will be placing the talisman on your altar, you can use something larger.

Place everything on your altar or a table or on a cloth on the floor. If you are doing this inside, you might want to put the stone on a plate or dish to contain any small mess.

Sprinkle the salt over the stone and say:

> *I bless this talisman with the power of earth*
> *so it might ground and strengthen me*
> *with the energy of my power animal.*

Sprinkle the water over the stone and say:

> *I bless this talisman with the power of water*
> *that I might flow gracefully and flexibly through my life.*

Waft the sage or incense over the stone or feather and say:

> *I bless this talisman with the power of air*
> *so that I might communicate clearly with my power animal*
> *and hear its wisdom when I need it.*

Light the green or brown candle and say:

> *I bless this talisman with the power of fire*
> *so that I will always have the bright spirit of my*
> *power animal to guide me through the darkness.*

Light the candle representing deity and say:

> *I ask the gods (or Bast or whichever deity you follow)*
> *to bless this talisman, that it might remind me always*
> *of the gift I have been given. So mote it be.*

Sit for a few minutes holding the stone and feel the energy that radiates from it, then snuff out the candle and put it someplace safe.

In the cat's eye, all things belong to the cat.

A Power Animal Meditation

This is a basic meditation to help you connect with your power animal. If you have problems with visualization, you can gaze at a picture or figure of your animal with your eyes partially closed. If you have soft, meditative music or drumming, play it in the background. You can do some research about the animal ahead of time or just see what comes to you.

Sit comfortably and either close your eyes or let them relax so they are partially closed. Focus on your power animal as you slow and deepen your breathing. Visualize it sitting in front of you, relaxed and alert, looking back at you with intelligence in its eyes. Feel your breathing synchronize with that of your power animal so you breathe in when it breathes in and you breathe out when it breathes out.

Flex your hands slightly, as if you were stretching out paws, and watch your power animal do the same. Open your mouth in a silent roar and see your power animal roar back at you. Feel its strength and dignity, and know that you are completely safe with it. Breathe together for a while and stay open for any messages it may have to share with you.

When the time feels right, thank it for its presence and come fully back to your daily life.

The Tyger

WILLIAM BLAKE

Tyger! Tyger! burning bright,
In the forests of the night,
What immortal hand or eye
Could frame thy fearful symmetry?

In what distant deeps or skies
Burnt the fire of thine eyes?
On what wings dare he aspire?
What the hand dare sieze the fire?

And what shoulder, & what art,
Could twist the sinews of thy heart?
And when thy heart began to beat,
What dread hand? & what dread feet?

What the hammer? what the chain?
In what furnace was thy brain?
What the anvil? what dread grasp
Dare its deadly terrors clasp?

When the stars threw down their spears,
And water'd heaven with their tears,
Did he smile his work to see?
Did he who made the Lamb make thee?

Tyger! Tyger! burning bright
In the forests of the night,
What immortal hand or eye
Dare frame thy fearful symmetry?

CHAPTER 11

Cat Divination

The smallest feline
is a masterpiece.

• • • • • • • • •
LEONARDO DA VINCI

• • •

You've probably already thought of a number of ways to practice magic with your cat, but you might not have realized that they can help you in the area of divination as well. Have you ever noticed how cats seem to know things before they happen? Mine always know when I am going to try catching them to put them in their carriers to go to the vet. It's an amazing feat. The carrier can have sat out for three days. The cat has been hanging around for the last hour. And yet, when you finally go to get the cat—vanished! It's magic.

Admittedly, this kind of predictive ability isn't all that helpful to you (it's kind of the reverse), but you can tap into that feline mental gift to assist you in your divination work. You know, as long as the cat is in the mood to do so.

Cat Tarot Decks

If you like to use tarot cards, there are a number of lovely decks out now that feature cats. I am particularly fond of my own deck, of course: *The Everyday Witch Tarot*, whose illustrations by the fabulous Elisabeth Alba are filled with witches, brooms, and cats of every size and color. She even added calico cats in the cups suit when I lost my beloved Samhain. It is like having my little cat immortalized in a thousand decks. (Naturally, there are black cats on a number of cards as well.) Another favorite is *Mystical Cats Tarot* (also from Llewellyn) by Lunaea Weatherstone and illustrator Mickie Mueller. I got that one just because I loved the artwork so much.

My pal Rebecca Elson, who reviews lots of tarot decks on her blog, *The Magical Buffet*, particularly liked a deck called *Cat's Eye Tarot* created by Debra M. Givin, a veterinarian. Givin does something a little unusual in that she has the cat colors represent the different suits: practical brown tabbies for pentacles, sweet black-and-white kitties for cups, talkative Siamese for swords, and flashy red tabbies for wands.

Elson also liked the *Bleu Cat Tarot* by Beth Seilonen, which features Siamese cats in lovely shades of blue.

Other cat-centric decks you can try include the following:

- *Tarot Familiars* by Lisa Parker
- *Black Cats Tarot* by Maria Kuara and Lo Scarabeo
- *Tarot of Pagan Cats* by Lo Scarabeo
  (also comes in a mini version)
- *CatTarot Deck* by Lo Scarabeo
- *Tarot of the Cat People* by Karen Kuykendall
- *Tarot of White Cats* by Lo Scarabeo

There are also some nice-looking cat oracle cards that I am going to have to try out, such as:

- *Cats Inspirational Oracle Cards* by Barbara Moore and Marco Turini
- *Spirit Cats Inspirational Card Deck* by Nicole Piar

Some of these are probably better used for admiring the beautiful artwork than they are for actual readings, but you will have to explore them for yourself to find out.

From Tales of the Mystical Cats
by Lunaea Weatherstone

THE SHIELD OF SEKHMET SPREAD

Sekhmet is one of our most revered deities, an Egyptian lioness goddess whose name means "the one who is powerful." In ancient Egypt she was invoked in times of war to ensure victory and celebrated in times of peace for her powers of healing and reconciliation. This three-card spread is based on a gold aegis, or breastplate shield, with a likeness of Sekhmet (ca. 900–750 BCE). Use this spread when you need to connect with the source of your own personal power.

　　1: What weakens you?

　　2: What strengthens you?

　　3: How can you best use your power?

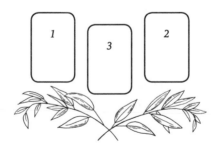

Divination with Your Cat

There are a number of ways you can do divination work with your cat, all of them fairly simple because, let's face it, the cat isn't going to do anything complicated. (Unless you want to try and read the future in mouse entrails…I sure don't.) And of course, all of these depend on the willing cooperation of your cat. Magic the Cat almost always shows up when I read tarot and helps whether I want her to or not (although sometimes she just comes up and lies on top of the entire spread, which I suspect she thinks is more helpful than it actually is). All you can do is invite the cat to take part and see what happens.

> *Tarot:* Shuffle a deck of tarot cards and place them face down on the table or the floor in a long row. Ask a question and see if the cat will choose a card either by touching it with their paw or sitting or lying in front of it. If you can't tell which of a few cards the cat may be indicating, pull those few out and try again with only those. Alternately, you can place all the cards face up in a loose pile.

> *Rune Stones:* Mix up the stones in a bag or bowl and then place them rune-side down on a table or the floor. Ask a question and see if the cat will pick one or a few. And yes, knocking them off the table and onto the floor counts.

Pendulum: Cats are naturally attracted to things hanging at the bottom of a string anyway. Pick a direction to indicate yes and one to indicate no, ask your question, and see if the cat will bat the pendulum in one direction or another.

Dream Divination: If you have a cat who sleeps by your pillow, as Magic the Cat does with me, you can ask for their help in dream divination and they might guide you once you fall asleep. You can also put a catnip sachet under your pillow since catnip is supposed to aid sleep.

You can also use felidomancy, otherwise known as ailuromancy (from the Greek *ailouros*, "cat"). Felidomancy is the practice of making predictions based on the behavior and actions of cats by observing their movements and even which way they jump.

There is a whole series of weather prediction superstitions based on cats, for instance. Rain is coming if your cat lies with its head against the floor or cleans its face from behind its ear. Storms are on the way if a cat places its forehead on the floor or leaps around wildly. (This one kind of makes sense, since cats can be more sensitive to impending weather changes.) Some believed that a cat turning its tail to the fire indicated a change in the weather, and wiggling its tail in the winter meant snow was coming. A cat scratching a table leg might mean a change in the weather too. Scratching frantically at the ground meant an earthquake was coming.

Cat behavior is said to predict other things as well. Ask your cat a question. If it yawns, that means an opportunity is coming your way. If it sneezes, that's a good omen, and if it runs away, a secret will soon be revealed (or the cat is bored…). If your cat meows in response to your question, it may be warning you of trouble.

A Spell for Divination

If you want to try some divination work with your cat (whether or not the kitty is a familiar), keep in mind that cats, just like people, are sometimes not in the right mood for predicting the future. But if the cat is willing to help, you can say this fast and simple spell to give your work together a boost.

> *Cat so smart and cat so wise*
> *Tell what it is you see*
> *Use your feline intuition*
> *Predict what lies ahead for me!*

For I Will Consider My Cat Jeoffry

CHRISTOPHER SMART

For I will consider my Cat Jeoffry.

For he is the servant of the Living God, duly and
daily serving him.

For at the first glance of the glory of God in the East
he worships in his way.

For is this done by wreathing his body seven times
round with elegant quickness.

For then he leaps up to catch the musk, which is the
blessing of God upon his prayer.

For he rolls upon prank to work it in.

For having done duty and received blessing he
begins to consider himself.

For this he performs in ten degrees.

For first he looks upon his forepaws to see if they are
clean.

For secondly he kicks up behind to clear away there.

For thirdly he works it upon stretch with the
forepaws extended.

For fourthly he sharpens his paws by wood.

For fifthly he washes himself.

For sixthly he rolls upon wash.

For seventhly he fleas himself, that he may not be interrupted upon the beat.

For eighthly he rubs himself against a post.

For ninthly he looks up for his instructions.

For tenthly he goes in quest of food.

For having considered God and himself he will consider his neighbor.

For if he meets another cat he will kiss her in kindness.

For when he takes his prey he plays with it to give it a chance.

For one mouse in seven escapes by his dallying.

For when his day's work is done his business more properly begins.

For he keeps the Lord's watch in the night against the adversary.

For he counteracts the powers of darkness by his electrical skin and glaring eyes.

For he counteracts the Devil, who is death, by
brisking about the life.

For in his morning orisons he loves the sun and the
sun loves him.

For he is of the tribe of Tiger.

For the Cherub Cat is a term of the Angel Tiger.

For he has the subtlety and hissing of a serpent,
which in goodness he suppresses.

For he will not do destruction if he is well-fed,
neither will he spit without provocation.

For he purrs in thankfulness when God tells him
he's a good Cat.

For he is an instrument for the children to learn
benevolence upon.

For every house is incomplete without him, and a
blessing is lacking in the spirit.

For the Lord commanded Moses concerning the cats
at the departure of the Children of Israel from
Egypt.

For every family had one cat at least in the bag.

For the English Cats are the best in Europe.

For he is the cleanest in the use of his forepaws of
any quadruped.

For the dexterity of his defense is an instance of the
love of God to him exceedingly.

For he is the quickest to his mark of any creature.

For he is tenacious of his point.

For he is a mixture of gravity and waggery.

For he knows that God is his Saviour.

For there is nothing sweeter than his peace when at
rest.

For there is nothing brisker than his life when in
motion.

For he is of the Lord's poor, and so indeed is he
called by benevolence perpetually–Poor Jeoffry!
poor Jeoffry! the rat has bit thy throat.

For I bless the name of the Lord Jesus that Jeoffry is
better.

For the divine spirit comes about his body to sustain
it in complete cat.

For his tongue is exceeding pure so that it has in
purity what it wants in music.

For he is docile and can learn certain things.

For he can sit up with gravity, which is patience
upon approbation.

For he can fetch and carry, which is patience in
employment.

For he can jump over a stick, which is patience upon
proof positive.

For he can spraggle upon waggle at the word of
command.

For he can jump from an eminence into his master's
bosom.

For he can catch the cork and toss it again.

For he is hated by the hypocrite and miser.

For the former is afraid of detection.

For the latter refuses the charge.

For he camels his back to bear the first notion of
business.

For he is good to think on, if a man would express
himself neatly.

For he made a great figure in Egypt for his signal
services.

For he killed the Icneumon rat, very pernicious by
land.

For his ears are so acute that they sting again.

For from this proceeds the passing quickness of his
attention.

For by stroking of him I have found out electricity.

For I perceived God's light about him both wax and
fire.

For the electrical fire is the spiritual substance which
God sends from heaven to sustain the bodies both
of man and beast.

For God has blessed him in the variety of his
movements.

For, though he cannot fly, he is an excellent
clamberer.

For his motions upon the face of the earth are more
than any other quadruped.

For he can tread to all the measures upon the music.

For he can swim for life.

For he can creep.

CHAPTER 12

Crafts & Recipes for You & Your Cat

When I play with my cat, how do I know that she is not passing time with me rather than I with her?

• • • • • •
MONTAIGNE

•   •   •

You might not think of crafts or recipes when it comes to your cat (except trying to keep them out of whichever one you're doing), but there are actually a few fun crafty things you can do with cat magic. Some of these call for ingredients from your cat (like fur, shed nails, and dropped whiskers) and some use cat-friendly herbs like catnip and valerian. As with everything else in the book, you can always vary things to suit you and your cat.

Most of these are cat magic for you, but a few of them are magic you do on behalf of your kitty.

Crafts & Crafty Spells

Cat Charm for Protection

Everyone knows how protective a cat can be of its home and territory and those that it loves. Tap into that protective energy with this simple charm that you can carry wherever you go.

Spell components: a cat charm or figure (this can be made out of anything you like—metal, stone, etc.—but it should have a loop you can use to hang it on a necklace or keychain), a sprig of rosemary or some dried rosemary, some sea salt (regular salt will do), and a shed cat's claw. If you can't find a claw your cat has shed, you can use the tip of a claw from when you trim kitty's nails. You will also need a small square of black or white cloth (it should be about the same size as your cat figure when the cloth is formed into a tiny bag), some black thread, and a sewing needle.

To create the charm, place the cat claw, a pinch of salt, and a few bits of rosemary into the middle of the cloth and sew it shut with the black thread. You should end up with a tiny bag or square. Then tie the bag around the cat figure's neck with the thread, looping it around enough times to make sure it is secure.

If you like, you can bless and consecrate it. Say, "With this cat charm, keep me from harm." Place the charm on a necklace, hang it from your keychain, or tuck it into your purse or wallet so it goes where you go.

Lucky Cat Blessings

The Japanese lucky cat with one paw raised, known as maneki neko, is a popular symbol for luck, success, and prosperity. If you want to draw those things into your life, you can make a miniature lucky cat altar.

Spell components: a maneki neko figurine (these can be found online and in many gift shops—it doesn't need to be fancy or expensive), a special coin (such as a half dollar or dollar coin, or an interesting foreign coin if you happen to have one), a small square of cloth to put underneath the cat and the other items. You may want to pick the color of the cloth to match the figurine or to coincide with the traditional cat colors, which have different meanings:

CALICO (ORANGE, BLACK, AND WHITE): traditional color combination, considered to be the luckiest

WHITE: happiness, purity, and positive things to come

GOLD: wealth and prosperity

BLACK: wards off evil spirits

RED: success in love and relationships

GREEN: good health

You'll also need three small tumbled stones (three is considered to be an auspicious number in Japanese culture, just as it is for witches); again, you can pick colors that match the traditional Japanese meanings or use one or more of the stones associated magically with luck, such as amber, aventurine, jet, tiger's-eye, or turquoise.

To create the altar, place the cloth under the figurine and put the coin and the three stones in front of it. (Traditionally these were placed in bedrooms or studies, but you can position yours anywhere that feels right.) If you are in need of luck or success, or if you have a particularly good day and want to say thank you, you can put a flower or some other offering in front of the altar.

Candle to Ward Off Evil

In China it was traditional to paint a cat's image onto lanterns to ward off evil influences. These days we tend not to be worried so much about the kind of evil they had in mind (bad spirits and such), but there is certainly a lot of bad stuff out there, and it can't hurt to have a little something extra to ward off, say, computer viruses and telemarketers. If you have artistic talent, you can paint a cat onto a lantern, but for most of us, it is best to stick with something simpler, like carving a cat figure or face into the side of a tall pillar candle.

Spell components: a black or white pillar candle and a fire-safe plate or candleholder to burn it on. A pointed tool to carve with, such as a toothpick, athame, or anything with a tip on it (you can probably find plenty of useful things in your kitchen drawers, but if you are using a knife, be very careful not to cut yourself). If you want to get really fancy, you can take a smaller candle, like a birthday candle, in another color, and once you have finished carving, heat it up enough so that you can drip the wax into the carved lines for contrast, so the cat shape stands out even more.

If you are not particularly artistic, don't worry: this is symbolic and doesn't have to be perfect. You can always practice ahead of time on a piece of paper or a candle you don't care about. It is also okay to print out a picture of a basic cat face or figure and copy it. Use your pointed object to carve the cat into one side of the candle. (Hint: if you mess it up, you can gently warm the wax and rub out your mistake.) If desired, light your smaller accent candle and drip a contrasting color into the carved lines. Place it on the plate or candleholder. Say:

> *Cat so mighty, cat so fierce*
> *Make a wall no evil can pierce.*

Cat Charm for Strength and Flexibility

One of the things we admire most about cats is their strength and flexibility. It sometimes seems as though they pull off some impossible feat every day. Push their way into someplace they shouldn't be able to get to? Piece of cake. Leap directly from the floor to the top of a bookshelf? Sure, why not. Faster than a speeding bullet when they are running away from the cat carrier before a vet visit? Every freaking time.

Which of us doesn't wish from time to time that we could be as strong and adaptable as our feline friends? Here's a simple charm to help with exactly that.

Like all magic, charms are about focus and intent. We take an object—in this case, a cat charm—and enchant it to be a focal point for our goal. Then that object serves as a reminder of our intent at the times when we need it most.

Spell components: a cat-shaped charm or small carved figurine made out of metal, wood, or stone (it can be an actual charm like the type you hang off a bracelet or something that you will make into a necklace that you can wear on the days when you most feel the need for strength and flexibility). You can even buy a ready-made necklace and simply enchant the entire thing. You will also need a cat whisker (if you can't find one, some fur or a shed claw will do), a black or brown candle, an athame or toothpick, and a piece of string or twine.

To make the charm, place the charm or figurine on your altar or a table. Take the candle and with your athame or a toothpick, carve the Norse rune symbol Uruz (which looks like an upside-down U with one leg shorter than the other) into the candle to represent strength. Put the whisker, fur, or claw underneath the candle to infuse it with the cat's energy. Light the candle and hold the charm over it. Say:

> *This charm is enchanted with the energy*
> *of feline strength and flexibility.*

Hold the charm in one hand and the knife in the other. Wave the knife over the charm, saying:

> *This charm is enchanted with strength.*

Put the knife down and pick up the string or twine. Wind it around the charm briefly and say:

> *This charm is enchanted with flexibility. When I wear or carry this*
> *charm, this strength and flexibility will be mine. So mote it be.*

Cat Home Blessing Charm Bag

It is truly a blessing to have a cat in your home, so why not take a little bit of that magical feline energy and use it to make a feline home blessing charm bag? The charm bag will be one part protection plus one part love, with a touch of magic thrown in for good measure.

Spell components: a bit of fur or some shed nails and whiskers from your cat or cats, a small quartz crystal, some rosemary and dried rose petals, plus a little catnip if you're going to be hanging the bag where the cat can't get at it. If you have one, a small picture of your cat is good, or you can draw a tiny cat picture on a piece of paper. You can use either a premade drawstring bag for this or create your own bag using a square of cloth (gold, silver, white, or blue) and a ribbon or piece of yarn. Optional: confetti stars and moons.

To make your blessing bag, place all the ingredients in the bag or in the middle of the cloth square, and then tie it closed. As you are placing each item, think about how blessed your house is to have the cat or cats that live within its walls. When the bag is completed, say:

> *Blessed am I to have this home*
> *And too the cat(s) within it*
> *Bless this place and keep it safe*
> *And all those who dwell in it.*

Hang the bag up near an entrance or over your altar.

Tarot Card for Strength and a Lion's Courage

One of my favorite tarot cards is Strength, which often pictures a woman standing with a lion who is clearly being loving and supportive. In the *Everyday Witch Tarot's* Strength card, we also added a small black cat. This is an easy way to create a symbol to remind you that you have more strength and courage (and allies) than you think.

Spell components: a Strength tarot card (make a photocopy of one from your deck or print one off of the internet). A frame or a piece of cardboard or poster board you can cut to fit the card. The frame needs at least half an inch of surface and should be flat since you are going to write on it. You will also need colored markers or crayons and white glue. Optional: Small tiger's-eye chips.

To make your strength reminder, place the card or print inside the frame or center it inside the paper you are using instead. Glue it into place if you are using a piece of paper. On the frame, write words like *strength, courage, I can do it, never give up,* and *I am not alone* with the markers, and draw cat faces, figures, or paw prints in between if you desire. If you are using the tiger's-eye chips, glue them into place around the edges of the frame or in between the words. Then hang it someplace where you will see it often.

Memento Box

When Samhain died, my friend Ellen suggested I clip a bit of her hair before I sent her body out for cremation. I'd never done so before, but I found it a great comfort in the first few weeks after she was gone. I kept it in a small white jewelry box I happened to have around and would actually open the box once or twice a day to stroke the little piece of fur. Eventually I no longer needed to do that, but the box is still there, next to the larger wooden box that holds her ashes and a picture of her when she was still alive. I did the same thing with Minerva's fur, but because I couldn't find a suitable box, I used a small cloth pouch instead.

It is easy to create a memento box for a beloved cat who has crossed the Rainbow Bridge, and you can do this in any way that suits your style and your budget. You can find a simple wooden box at most craft stores or possibly even at a thrift store. Plus, of course, there's always the internet. I found a plain wooden "memory box" on Amazon for less than ten dollars that was specifically designed for this kind of craft. Of course, you can also use a nice cardboard box if you happen to have a sturdy one with no decorations or writing on it.

Spell components: gather any of the following items to decorate the outside: a picture or pictures of your cat, pieces of fabric cut from their favorite blanket or cloth toys, pictures or drawings of food or things they liked to play with, tiger's-eye beads or chips, anything else that reminds you of the cat, a picture of a rainbow or a bridge or wherever you envision them now, even drawings or pictures of mice, if the cat would have liked that. Decorative ribbon or cord. Glue. Optional: markers or crayons or a wood-burning tool. For the inside, any special mementos of your cat, including pictures, a clipping of their fur, a favorite toy, their collar if they wore one, or even their ashes if you have them.

To make a memento box, arrange all the items you are using to decorate the box and glue them into place. It is nice to do this slowly and mindfully, remembering the cat with joy and love as you work. You can write the cat's name on the box (or print it out in fancy script on the computer ahead of time and then glue it on) or burn it into the box if you happen to have a wood-burning tool. Once the box is finished, place any mementos inside and put the box on your altar or any other safe place.

Cat Footprint for Remembrance

I know a few people who sent their animals out for cremation and got back not only their pet's ashes, but also a medallion with an imprint of the animal's paw, much as you see sometimes done with a baby's hand- or footprints. There's no reason you can't do this at home, either before or after your cat passes.

Spell components: a package of self-hardening clay (again, I found this on Amazon for under ten dollars; you can probably find it in a local craft store), a ribbon, a small tool to shape the clay (a kitchen knife or a screwdriver will work). Optional: a pointed tool with which to write on the clay.

If you are doing this while your cat is still alive, be sure to wipe the clay completely from the cat's foot when you are done, even though most self-drying clays are nontoxic. Form a piece of clay into a medallion shape, either round or oval or teardrop. Press the cat's paw gently into the clay until it makes an impression. Using a tool, poke a hole through the top so you can put the ribbon through it later, after it dries. If desired, write the cat's name in the clay either over or underneath the paw print.

Herbal Charm Bag for Your Cat

Unlike the previous crafts, which were designed for you, the next few are created with your kitty in mind. This herbal charm bag is a general all-around good-vibes-for-the-cat type of thing. You can make one bag for all the cats in your house or you can make a charm bag for each cat.

Spell components: a plain muslin drawstring bag (you can find these in the kitchen section or at health food stores) or a square of white or unbleached cloth and a needle and thread, a black marker or various colored markers, dried catnip or valerian, a tumbled tiger's-eye or a piece of quartz crystal too large for a cat to swallow (or leave the stone out of the bag and just set the finished bag on top of the stone for a while to absorb the energy).

To make the charm bag, on the bag or cloth write the name of the cat or cats plus all the good things you wish for them, such as health, long life, fun, lots of naps, etc. You can also decorate it with rune symbols, hearts, or whatever you like. Put the herbs and the stone inside the bag and pull the ties tight, then knot them a few times so the bag won't open. If you are using the square of cloth, place the herbs and stone inside, then fold it in half so there are three open sides and one closed side. Carefully sew the open edges shut so you are left with a small sachet (it doesn't have to look neat or pretty, so don't worry if you are not a professional seamstress).

When you are done, hold it tight and think about how much you love your cat. If you want, you can bless and consecrate it on your altar or leave it out under the next full moon. Then let the kitty have it!

Charmed Bell for Your Cat's Protection

If your cat wears a collar (especially if they go outside), you can make this simple charmed bell to keep them safe. It will also help to protect the local birds if the cat goes out, which isn't a bad thing either.

Spell components: a small bell that can be securely attached to the cat's collar, a small plate, a sage smudge stick, small bowls of salt and water, a white or black candle. Optional: a picture of the cat. This is a good craft to do on the night of the full moon.

To make the charmed bell, place the bell in the middle of the plate on your altar or on the ground outside if you are doing it under the moonlight. Put the picture, if you're using one, where you can see it. Light the candle, then light the sage smudge stick and waft it over the bell to fill it with the power of air. Sprinkle the salt over the bell (earth), followed by the water (water). Then hold the bell over the candle—high enough up so you don't get burned! (We want the power of fire, not blisters.) Then say:

> *Moon, moon, up above*
> *Bless this bell for the cat I love*
> *Keep him safe from hurt and harm*
> *With the magic of this charm!*

Then attach the bell to the kitty's collar.

Bespelled Statue for Your Cat's Protection and Health

In witchcraft we sometimes use an object to stand in for a person—for instance, when we make a poppet that symbolizes a friend who is in need of healing, and do magic for healing on the poppet instead of the actual person. This craft is a variation on that practice, except in this case you will be using a cat statue or a Bast statue to symbolize your cat. (It will be a whole lot easier to get the statue to sit still, for one thing.) Essentially, we will be putting a spell of protection and health on the statue, which will then represent your kitty. If you are crafty, you can make a statue out of clay or carve one out of wood. If you're not, feel free to buy one that someone else has made.

Spell components: a cat or Bast statue (this doesn't need to be large), a piece of agate or red jasper, a piece of paper and a pen, a sprig of fresh rosemary or a small amount of dried herb, fresh or dried lavender, salt, water, and a sage smudge stick. You will also need a white candle in a candleholder—if your statue is small, you may want to use a tiny candle like a tealight or a chime candle.

To make the bespelled statue, write the cat's name on the piece of paper and put it under the statue. Place the candle in front of the statue and light it. Light the sage and waft it over the statue to symbolize clearing any negative energy away from the cat (you can sage yourself too while you're at it—what the heck). Sprinkle the statue with salt and water, then say:

Bast, I make these offerings in your name and
ask that you bespell this statue to keep my cat from harm.

Place the agate or jasper in front of the statue and say:

A magical stone for protection and health.

Brush the statue with the rosemary sprig or sprinkle the dried herb on it, then do the same with the lavender. Say:

These blessed herbs for protection and health.

Kiss the statue, then say:

All my love and my heartfelt wishes
for my cat's continued health and protection.

Hold your hands up to the sky, then say:

Bast, bless this statue and the cat it represents.

Sit for a moment and feel the energy of the charmed statue, and then place it on your altar or somewhere else safe. Periodically light the candle and envision the cat being surrounded by white, protective light.

> *A cat is a puzzle for which*
> *there is no solution.*
>
> **HAZEL NICHOLSON**

Recipes

Some people make food for their cats at home on a regular basis because of dietary issues or a dislike of storebought brands, some of which are filled with a lot of things that aren't necessarily good for cats. (My favorite is "chicken byproduct meal," which can be made from pretty much anything on the chicken.) Most of us, however, can't manage to take things that far and settle for buying the best food we can find and afford. Making homemade food for cats can be involved and time consuming, and you do need to pay attention to the nutritional balance in anything you are feeding as a regular meal, so it isn't for everyone.

That doesn't mean you can't occasionally whip up a special treat for your favorite felines, however. Note that all treats should be used within one week of making. Keep in mind that certain people foods aren't good for cats (like chocolate, onions, bacon or other pork products, or bones), although Magic the Cat tells me that the occasional piece of cheese never hurt anyone.

Fish Straws

Mix ¾ cup low or no-salt canned tuna or salmon mashed up with ¼ cup water, 1 cup whole wheat flour, and 1 tablespoon butter (not margarine). Pinch off a chunk and roll it between your hands to make a long, thin piece, like a cheese straw or straight pretzel, and place the pieces on an ungreased cookie sheet. Bake in a 300-degree oven for about 25 minutes or until lightly browned. Makes about 24. Refrigerate the leftovers.

Catnip and Cheese Balls

Cream together 2 tablespoons butter, 1 egg white, ½ cup grated mild cheese (like cheddar), and ½ teaspoon catnip. When well mixed, add in ½ cup flour. Roll into 12 balls and bake on an ungreased cookie sheet for about 35 minutes in a 250-degree oven. These are rich, so only feed one at a time and store the rest in the refrigerator or gift a few to another cat-loving friend.

Beef Snack Bites

Combine 3 ounces finely ground beef, 2 tablespoons oatmeal, and 1 beaten egg. If you want, you can add a little catnip to this too. Press it out flat onto a lightly oiled pan and bake for 6–8 minutes at 350 degrees or until crisp. After it cools, break into small pieces. Refrigerate leftovers in a tightly closed container.

Grain-Free Dehydrated Treats

For those who are feeding a grain-free diet, if you have a dehydrator, it is easy to make simple treats using one ingredient—meat or fish (like salmon, but be sure to take the skin off because it is too greasy to dry well). It will take seven to ten hours, depending on the size of the pieces you are using, and the treats must be refrigerated afterward. But at least you know what's in them!

Dogs eat. Cats dine.

ANN TAYLOR

A NOTE FROM

Magic the Cat

Cats are not very far removed from our wild ancestors. That's a good thing to keep in mind when giving us treats. (You know you want to.) Things that are made from meat and fish are good, although you'll want to make sure there are no bones in either. Contrary to all the pictures of cats drinking bowls of cream, we don't really digest milk well— although that won't stop us from stealing yours if you leave the cereal bowl where we can get at it. A little piece of cheese is okay, though, or a tiny amount of yogurt, as long as your kitty doesn't have digestive issues. Stay away from artificial additives because ewwww. And if you don't want to worry about making food from scratch, most cats are perfectly happy with treats from a bag. Mind you, the ones we like this week we'll probably turn our noses up at next week, but that's just to keep you on your toes.

CHAPTER 13

Channeling Your Inner Cat

The ideal of calm exists

in a sitting cat.

· · · · · · ·

JULES RENARD

• • •

Most cat lovers have at least a part of them that secretly—or not so secretly—would like to be a cat. Who doesn't want to be able to prowl under the moonlight or curl up in the sun and nap? If we're very, very good, we might come back in our next lives as the spoiled cats of loving witches, but for now here are a few spells to help you channel your own inner cat. You can ask your familiar to help lend their energy to these, but note that none of these spells needs anything other than your focus and intention.

Cat Naps

Many people—me included—don't get enough sleep and often don't sleep well even when we do. My remedy for that is to take a short nap most days. It's just for about forty-five minutes, but it is enough to give me a second wind and enable me to spend the evening writing books like this. Of course, one of the best things about my naps is that I almost always have company when I take them. Like any sensible cats, mine are all about the naps. Magic usually curls up right by my head and Mystic sleeps by my feet. It's lovely.

So learn from your cat and take a nap—or, at the very least, do this simple spell to help you sleep better, whether you do it at night or in the middle of the afternoon in a nice patch of sunlight.

Cat naps, cat naps, sleep, sleep, sleep
Help me get some rest so deep
Like the cat who sleeps at will
Make my nighttime calm and still
Restful sleep for body and mind
So every day I can unwind.

Independence

One of the things cat people love about their animals is how independent they are. Dogs are much more likely to hover at your feet and beg for attention. Cats, on the other hand, will demand attention if they're in the mood for it and ignore you the rest of the time. Kind of a mixed blessing, really.

I'm not suggesting you ignore the people in your life, but cats do set a good example in their ability to stand on their own, proudly self-sufficient (until they need to open a can, that is). If you feel as though you would like to be a little more independent, try saying this spell. If your cat is feeling cooperative, she might even say it with you.

Bast, so proud and independent
Help me be more like my cat
Standing on my own strong feet
Standing firm and standing pat
Lend me feline strength of will
And courage to be on my own
Tough and steadfast like a kitty
Good with others, good alone.

Remembering to Play

Most of us spend a lot of our time working. Sometimes it is hard to remember that it is just as important to take time out to play and have fun—unless you are lucky enough to have a cat around to remind you.

If you are someone who is always working and hardly ever stops to just do things because you enjoy them, try this spell so you'll remember to take the time to play.

Cat, my cat, help me to see
That work all day won't balance me
Play's important for people too
So let's go play, me and you!

She sights a Bird—she chuckles

EMILY DICKINSON

She sights a Bird—she chuckles—
She flattens—then she crawls—
She runs without the look of feet—
Her eyes increase to Balls—

Her Jaws stir—twitching—hungry—
Her Teeth can hardly stand—
She leaps, but Robin leaped the first—
Ah, Pussy, of the Sand,

The Hopes so juicy ripening—
You almost bathed your Tongue—
When Bliss disclosed a hundred Toes—
And fled with every one—

In Summary

*Authors like cats because they are such
quiet, loveable, wise creatures, and cats
like authors for the same reason.*

• • • • • • • •
ROBERTSON DAVIES

• • •

Now that you have read this book from cover to cover (or skimmed it for the bits you wanted), you know everything there is to know about practicing magic with and for cats.

Just kidding.

The truth is, we never stop learning about our cats or from them. This is one of the joys of sharing your life with a companion of the feline persuasion—they always have something to teach us, whether it is about magic or cats or even being human. Of course, you have to be paying attention to learn the lessons, but I'm sure you are doing that. If not, your cat will probably help to focus your mind with a sharp claw or an obliging nip.

Cats are truly the most magical of creatures. They are beautiful, smart, cunning, amusing, comforting, loving, and oh so mysterious. If you feed them and care for them, they will reward you with years of companionship—completely on their terms, of course, but you wouldn't expect anything else.

And if you are very lucky, you may end up with that particularly magical cat, a familiar, to share your witchy life along with your mundane one. But familiar or not, each and every cat brings its own special magic to our lives—for which I, for one, am incredibly grateful.

May you have nine lives, and may you share them all with some wonderful furry friends.

Blessings,

Deborah (and Magic the Cat)

A Note from Deborah

Books are written long before they come out—often a year or a year and a half ahead. At the time I wrote this, Magic the Cat was alive and well, and bossing me (and her sick brother) around. Sadly, I lost her and Mystic within eight days of each other at the beginning of this year—Magic on January 3, 2018, and Mystic on January 12, one day after their sixteen birthday.

I can't express how broken my heart is or how much I miss them, especially Magic the Cat, Queen of the Universe, who was so much more than just a companion. She was the first (and so far only) true familiar I have ever had, and she was a part of everything I did. I miss them both, but there is a huge gaping hole where that small black cat used to be.

Still, I am grateful for every day of the almost sixteen years I had them. They were a gift from the gods, and as hard as it was to see this book come out without Magic by my side, I am consoled by the fact that these last bits of wisdom are her legacy—one last book about the magic of cats from Magic the Cat. It is only fitting.

Cats are kindly masters,
just so long as you
remember your place.

PAUL GRAY

Recommended Reading

Magical Cat Books

Conway, D. J. *The Mysterious, Magickal Cat*. Woodbury, MN: Llewellyn, 1998, 2018.

Dugan, Ellen. *The Enchanted Cat: Feline Fascinations, Spells & Magick*. Woodbury, MN: Llewellyn, 2006.

Dunwich, Gerina. *Your Magickal Cat: Feline Magick, Lore, and Worship*. New York: Citadel Press, 2000.

Nahmad, Claire. *Catspells: A Collection of Enchantments for You and Your Feline Companion*. Philadelphia, PA: Running Press, 1993.

Telesco, Patricia. *Cat Magic: Mews, Myths, and Mystery*. Rochester, VT: Destiny Books, 1999.

Weatherstone, Lunaea, and Mickie Mueller. *Mystical Cats Tarot*. Woodbury, MN: Llewellyn, 2014.

Useful General Information on Cats

Eckstein, Warren, and Fay Eckstein. *How to Get Your Cat to Do What You Want: A Loving Way to Teach Your Cat How to Sit, Take Walks, Stop Scratching the Furniture, and Be Your Best Friend.* New York: Fawcett Books, 1990.

Fields-Babineau, Miriam. *Cat Training in 10 Minutes.* Neptune, NJ: TFH, 2003.

Frazier, Anitra, with Norma Eckroate. *The Natural Cat: The Comprehensive Guide to Optimum Care.* New York: Plume, 2008.

Galaxy, Jackson, and Kate Benjamin. *Catification: Designing a Happy and Stylish Home for Your Cat (and You!).* New York: Tarcher, 2014.

Johnson-Bennet, Pam. *Cat vs. Cat: Keeping Peace When You Have More Than One Cat.* New York: Penguin, 2004.

Taylor, David. *You & Your Cat: A Complete Guide to the Health, Care & Behavior of Cats.* New York: Alfred A Knopf, 1986.

Zucker, Martin. *The Veterinarian's Guide to Natural Remedies for Cats: Safe and Effective Alternative Treatments and Healing Techniques from the Nation's Top Holistic Veterinarians.* New York: Three Rivers Press, 1999.

Just For Fun (Some Silly Cat Books)

Gethers, Peter, and Norman Stiles (illustrations by William Bramhall). *Historical Cat*. New York: Ballantine, 1996.

Laland, Stephanie. *51 Ways to Entertain Your Housecat While You're Out: Easy-to-Make Toys and Games Guaranteed to Keep Your Pet Busy and Happy*. New York: Avon, 1984.

Lovka, Bob (illustrations by Setsu Broderick). *The Splendid Little Book of All Things Cat*. Irvine, CA: Bowtie Press, 1998.

Marciuliano, Francesco. *I Could Pee on This and Other Poems by Cats*. San Francisco, CA: Chronicle Books, 2012.

A Bit of History

Engels, Donald. *Classical Cats: The Rise and Fall of the Sacred Cat*. New York: Routledge, 1999.

Geyer, Georgie Anne. *When Cats Reigned Like Kings: On the Trail of the Sacred Cats*. Kansas City, MO: Andrews McMeel, 2004.

Saunders, Nicholas J. *The Cult of the Cat*. London: Thames and Hudson, 1991.

Trumble, Kelly (illustrations by Laszlo Kubinyi). *Cat Mummies*. New York: Clarion Books, 1965.

As every cat owner knows,
nobody owns a cat.

ELLEN PERRY BERKELEY

To order, call 1-877-new-wrld or visit llewellyn.com

Prices subject to change without notice

The Everyday Witch Tarot Kit

Deborah Blake
art by Elizabeth Alba

A fun, practical, easy-to-use tarot kit for every witch. Charming images pair with simple explanations to make this the go-to deck for anyone seeking to learn or practice the tarot. Based on the classic Rider-Waite deck but updated for the busy modern witch, this tarot has a whimsical air while still being dedicated to the serious job of providing answers to life's tough questions. Author Deborah Blake brings her friendly, approachable style to a tarot experience that's focused on the positive.

978-0-7387-4634-0

5.25 x 8

*boxed kit with 264-page full-color guidebook,
78 cards, and magnetic-closure box*